Screenplays as Literature Ser

Epics

1

THE LAST KNIGHT

An Historical Epic Movie Script
About the Siege of Malta in 1565

Original Screenplay
by
Brian James Godawa

The Last Knight: An Historical Epic Movie Script About the Siege of Malta in 1565
Screenplays as Literature Series • Epics • 1
1st Edition

Cover images used under license from Shutterstock.com.

Embedded Pictures Publishing
Los Angeles, CA
brian@embeddedpictures.com
www.embeddedpictures.com

ISBN: 978-1-942858-48-5 (paperback)
ISBN: 978-1-942858-49-2 (ebook)

Get Brian Godawa's Latest Movie Reviews, Updates, Discount Offers at HollywoodWorldviews.com.

HollywoodWorldviews.com

iv

Table of Contents

How to Read a Screenplay

The essential purpose of a screenplay is to be a blueprint out of which a movie is made. For this reason, screenplays or scripts are technically unfinished "works in progress." Movies are ultimately complex productions that are built from that blueprint that not only add the visual and audible aspects, but involve dozens of other creative artists' input, from the director to the actors to the costume designers, set designers and more. It has been said that there are three movies: the movie that is written in the script, the movie that is shot and the movie that is edited. That is because each step of that process involves creative input and changes that shape the movie into its final form. That final form is sometimes a faithful adaptation of the original screenplay, and sometimes a very different creature altogether.

Many movies are adapted from books or other sources, but when it comes to "spec scripts" or scripts written on speculation by a writer (with the hope that he can sell it after it is written), it all begins with the script. As the mighty Steven Spielberg once said, "If it ain't on the page, it ain't on the stage." It is the script that launches the ship, it is the script that draws and even guides the producers, the director, the actors and many others. Like a blueprint for a building that draws contractors, carpenters, electricians and more to construct the final edifice.

A spec script is the first embodiment of the story that grabs the hearts and imaginations of its readers, that inspires them to get the resources together to make it into a movie. And the power of that blueprint is its ability to convey an entertaining story. In Hollywood, as in most of life, story is king.

But because a screenplay is a blueprint, it is a kind of unfinished "outline" for a movie. It does not convey many details like a novel can. For instance, a script gives brief descriptions of characters, and only passing references to locations where events take place. Casting, costuming, set design as well as music and other elements will all be added to the movie by other professionals who expand that original story into a multilayered existential work of art.

Apart from the use of some narration, a movie script does not delve much into the inner mental thoughts of characters. It is more external than a novel. More visual and active, because the final movie form will be visual and active. That is, the reader must infer what is going on inside the characters based on their behavior, choices and words.

Also, a screenplay must cover story ground in less time than other mediums like novels. For example, good dialogue is usually shorter, more economical, it communicates more in fewer words, driven in part by the fact that a movie is about one-and-a-half to two hours long which translates to roughly 120 pages in a script (1 page per minute of final screen time). And as you will see, those pages are not full of text like a book is. Everything is shorter, briefer, more concise, similar to how short stories are compared to novels.

In this sense, a screenplay reader must be more sophisticated and attentive in their reading. Every scene, every gesture, every visual reference, every word must have a purpose in a screenplay. And all of it ideally integrates into the meaning that the storyteller is conveying. Now, there are exceptions to all these things, but my main concern is to help prepare the reader of this series to read a bit differently than usual.

Because of this abbreviated "external" approach to storytelling, reading a script requires active engagement on the part of the reader, who must sometimes decipher meanings, symbols, and character motivations like a detective. But the effort is well worth it as the reader becomes more skilled at watching movies and television with greater appreciation.

So, the strength of a movie script is that it is the essence of the story, its heart and soul, the primal foundation upon which a movie is built and expanded. That is why I am publishing the Screenplays as Literature Series, because despite the format being an abbreviated starting point, it is still a powerful way to tell a great story, indeed, to visualize a movie before it is made.

Reading a screenplay can be like watching a movie in your mind.

Why This Series?

Most of the screenplays in the Screenplays as Literature Series are unproduced. That means they have not been sold or made into movies. One might therefore conclude that they are not very good stories if they could not garner the interest of producers to buy them.

I will let the reader be the final arbiter of that decision. But let me at least make the argument that it is also equally possible that there is plenty of other reasons why these screenplays could be very good stories and yet still not produced.

Everyone in Hollywood knows that there are too many excellent scripts that don't get made. Sometimes it's because they don't recognize truly unique genius (the secret desire of every writer). With the studio blockbuster mentality, many producers and studios are looking for "more of the same" to make big money fast: prequels, sequels, rip-offs and spin-offs. Many great movies, like Schindler's List and Forrest Gump had a history of being rejected by every major studio in town and taking as long as ten or more years to get made—by the biggest producers in town!

In Hollywood there are a million bad reasons why good scripts don't get sold or made. It could be political incorrectness or other "social justice" censorship, it could be budget, it could be scheduling conflicts, it could be sea changes at studios, it could be creative differences or infighting. Often, it's the worst reason in the world, and the most common: You don't know the right people at the right time.

It's actually a miracle that any movie gets made. So, a lot of good ones languish unread or unproduced on the shelves of writers and others who just couldn't get people to see their scripts were undiscovered Oscar winners. I say that, not sarcastically, but with full sincerity. I believe it. Although, I would have to walk back the "Oscar" praise, since the Academy Awards have increasingly become less a sign of recognized excellence and more a sign of inbred political incest.

There is something called "The Blacklist" every year that is a list of recent scripts in Hollywood that are considered excellent by many readers, that have made the rounds, that everyone "in the know" has read, that are excellent, but yet never get made for a multitude of these very reasons listed above.

So, the point is that "unproduced" does not necessarily mean "bad." Sadly, that means that both the genius and the self-deluded amateur are in the same boat. Neither of them knows if their rejected script is an undiscovered masterpiece or a rejected delusion of mediocrity.

Am I an undiscovered Mozart or am I simply Salieri?

Again, I will let you the reader decide when it comes to the scripts in this series.

I just hope you enjoy these stories as much as I enjoyed writing them.

Understanding the Format

I will describe how to understand some of the unique formatting of a screenplay to help avoid confusion for the reader not acquainted with script formatting.

My first and foremost advice is to try to picture yourself watching a movie as you read the text. This is, after all, a script for a movie. So why not read it that way? You will have to imagine a lot of details to fill in the gaps of what costume designers, make-up artists, set designers and others would normally bring to the production of the script. But some readers actually like doing that.

Maybe a character may remind you of your favorite actor. So, imagine that actor as you read their action and dialogue. But notice every detail, every nuance of dialogue, because, as I noted earlier, every single detail is there for a reason.

Though I have formatted these screenplays basically as they were written, I have made some changes to make it easier for readers who are not in the film business. Normally, screenplays are written in courier font. Courier is an ugly font, so in the print version of this script I changed it to a more legible one that most readers will be comfortable with. I want to make it easier for you, not harder.

If you are reading this in ebook format, you can alter the font and spacing, to whatever format you want to read it in.

But let's get going with our quick lesson on how to read a script.

Scene Headings

After reading, "FADE IN," the reader will first notice what is called a "Scene Heading." It looks something like this:

INT. DUNGEON CORRIDOR – NIGHT

This is the notation of the location where the next scene is taking place. It helps the moviemakers organize for their shooting, but for the reader, it tells us quickly where the scene takes place.

The first element will either be "**INT**." which stands for interior, or "**EXT**." which stands for exterior. So, we know if we are inside a location or outside.

The next element of the scene heading is the actual location, such as "**DUNGEON CORRIDOR**." It is the briefest way of referring to that location. If there is some description in the paragraph below it, it will be very sparse, like painting a quick emotional picture of the feel of where we are, as opposed to wordy detailed descriptions. So, you will have to conjure up in your own mind what it looks like, like the set designer and costume designer does later. Hey, you'll be like a movie director!

Then we have "**NIGHT**" or "**DAY**." These are also quick designations for the shooting schedule, but they also tell us as readers what part of a day we are in.

Sometimes, the scene headings are shortened. If you already established "EXT... DAY" and then follow the character walking into the house, you need to alert the reader that he is now in "INT," but you don't have to necessarily add "DAY" again, because it was a continuous movement. So be prepared for some shortened scene headings to make the reading flow smoother.

Action

Usually below that scene heading is what is called the "action." Here is what it looks like with a scene heading before it:

INT. DUNGEON CORRIDOR - NIGHT

TWO CLOAKED FIGURES slither through the shadows of a medieval dungeon corridor. SCREAMS of torture. Rats SQUEAL.

Action describes any actions of characters we will see. Again, it is sparse and to the point and focused on what we are going to see on the screen, not what is in the character's head. Every word counts.

And because of that economy of language, do not expect grammar that follows the Chicago Manual of Style. Sentence fragments often rule the day because they keep the pace moving, like you are watching a movie, rather than reading a novel.

Sometimes a writer may add a stylistic flourish and tell us what the reader should conclude based on what we are seeing. So, you might see something like, "He obviously doesn't want to go with her." This is internal and might only be conveyed in the facial gesture of the actor. But since we cannot see the actors in the script, writers must sometimes cheat to help the reader understand what the viewer of the movie will be more capable of seeing.

You will notice the ALL CAPS words. Usually, when a character shows up for the first time anywhere in the script, their names are in all caps. It is a way of easily finding them for the movie makers, but it also helps the reader realize a new presence in the story.

Also, as in the example above, special effects, such as sounds or visual effects, are also capitalized to bring notice to the filmmakers for their production purposes. For the reader, this alerts us to the importance of a sound or image that would be more obvious to a movie viewer than a script reader.

This goes for underlined words as well. Underlining is like focusing the camera on something.

Sometimes, the scene headings and action can be used in a simpler format to differentiate complex action or visuals within a single location. You want it to read easily and quickly so you get a sense of the pace of the scene and aren't slowed down by details. Here is an example:

SLOW MOTION SHOT

Dragut's warhorse breaks through the cloud of smoke and fighting. He sees La Valette against a flagpole.

STARKEY AND THE MONSTER

Back up against the wall. A whack by the Monster snaps one of Starkey's swords in two.

LA VALETTE AND DRAGUT

battle around the flagpole. With a CLANG, their blades cross against the pole and freeze, straining against each other.

In this example, we are in one location, and two fights are going on that would be easily edited visually to follow for the audience. But for the reader, I tell them that first, they see a SLOW MOTION SHOT of the bad guy Dragut arriving. Then we jump over to a battle between the two characters STARKEY AND THE MONSTER, and then a jump back to Dragut who is now fighting the character LaValette.

Sometimes you might see something like this:

SUPER: ISTANBUL, TURKEY

This is called a "super" and it is short for "superimposed." It's basically like those titles we see at the bottom of the screen when we are introduced to a new location or to some introductory material like that famous screen-crawl at the beginning of each Star Wars movie.

Dialogue

When characters speak in a script, this is what it looks like:

GUARD
Ho. Where does ye think yer goin'?
(beat)
Ya looks shady to me.

The character's name is in all caps, so we clearly know who is speaking from what is being said. Before a character speaks, they must be described as present in the action first. Otherwise, they are popping in like a quantum fluctuation, which would be confusing to us Newtonian readers :-).

But also notice the word "beat" in parentheses. These are called, quite helpfully, "parentheticals," and they are used for several purposes. The word "beat" above, simply means a meaningful pause. It will affect the context of the words spoken or indicates a change of direction in dialogue. You can imagine the character pausing before they say their next lines, which adds nuance to the dialogue.

You might also read parentheticals with descriptions like "sarcastic," or "angrily," or something similar.

> JANE
> (sarcastic)
> Don't you look pretty.

This is done when the words themselves may not obviously communicate to the reader what a viewer can see on the screen. "Don't you look pretty" could be either genuine or sarcastic and you might not be able to determine that unless you saw the actress saying it with her facial gestures. So, the writer cheats a bit to help us catch what we cannot see.

You might also read an action in the parenthetical like "(To the other guy)" or "(he looks closer)." These would be used to describe actions done in the middle of talking, such as changing the character to whom they are talking.

Sometimes, you might see the unique parentheticals, (O.S.) and (V.O.) after the character name rather than below it:

> JOHN (O.S.)
> Put that gun down.

> JANE (V.O.)
> I realized John was not everything he said he was.

(O.S.) means "off-screen." It means that we hear the voice of the character, but we do not see them as we are watching the "movie in our minds." They are outside the camera view, but still in the scene.

(V.O.) means "voice-over," and is used when the character's voice is a narrator that is not within the actual story but is commenting upon it from outside the story. It's narration.

Well, there it is, your quick lesson on script-reading. It's not much different than reading plays. If you know the basic elements, it becomes quite easy to watch the movie in your mind as you read the script!

Introduction to The Last Knight Screenplay

My favorite movies have always been historical epics like Braveheart. So, when I discovered this story about the Knights of Malta versus the Turks of the Ottoman Empire in 1565, I saw it as Braveheart x 10. I just had to tell this story to the world.

Here is the pitch for the movie:

The Last Knight

Historical Epic

A true story. In 1565, Europe is on the brink of war with the Turkish Ottoman Empire. In England, a lone knight flees persecution only to discover that the island he has fled to is about to be invaded by an army of 40,000 Turks. Together with his 70-year old courageous Grand Master, they lead a small band of 600 knights, overcoming impossible odds to save the island — or Western Civilization will be destroyed forever.

I did research for this script as in-depth as I would for any novel. I read first-hand accounts in ancient books as well as well-known historian literature. Most of the characters and their stories in here are based on real people in history. I may have taken the most liberty with the lead character, Oliver Starkey, and I also obviously had to shorten timelines and telescope a lot of material, as well as other plot elements for creative license. But I believe it does capture the spirit of the true story as well as many of the amazing details. Some of the most amazing occurrences really happened.

What drew me to the story became one of the themes of the script that is still relevant for today, namely tolerance. Tolerance is a powerful value that touches everything. It is the tolerance of Western Civilization versus the intolerance of encroaching Islamic empire. But it also wrestles with the nuance of truth that requires some intolerance or we descend into the insanity of post-modernity that we now live with. Relativism leads to self-destruction, both philosophically and socially.

In the script, I deal with Christian vs. Muslim, Protestant vs. Roman Catholic, faith vs. unbelief, ancient vs. modernity. I tried to be fair and honest about the fact that both sides of a conflict are often intolerant of the other. So, how does truth come out? Are all sides equivalent? Can persons of different faith overcome their differences and fall in love? Can Protestants and Catholics unite against a common enemy? Is the Inquisition that different from Islamic jihad? Can Christianity and Islam co-exist or does Islamic imperialism threaten that hope?

The events of this sixteenth century period fall into a time of great change.

Chivalry and its knights were dying out as modernity overcame the old world with science, reason and Machiavellian ethics. The Teutons and Templars had been all but wiped out, and only the Knights Hospitallers were left, mostly because they were devoted to compassionate medical service. As the Reformation swept across Europe, threatening the Inquisitional grip of the Roman Catholic Church, the Ottoman empire was sweeping over the rest of the world, threatening to destroy all Christianity and the advance of Western Civilization.

It was truly the physical and ideological clash of civilizations. The victor would determine the fate of the world.

As the reader can see, all these issues are very relevant for today as Western Civilization is again under assault, not merely from Islamic Supremacy, but within its own ranks by the results of modernity turning on itself. And that is the power of a good historic epic tale, it sheds light on the present through lessons from the past.

The goal of telling an historical epic story is to help us avoid repeating history.

I hope The Last Knight will be one of those lessons that we all will learn from. If we don't, there may be no history left to repeat.

Brian James Godawa
Author and Screenwriter, *The Last Knight*

"THE LAST KNIGHT"

FADE IN:

INT. DUNGEON CORRIDOR - NIGHT

TWO CLOAKED FIGURES slither through the shadows of a medieval dungeon corridor. SCREAMS of torture. Rats SQUEAL.

A GRITTY JAILOR stands before a cell door. The figures pull back out of sight around the corner.

INT. DUNGEON CELL

SIR OLIVER STARKEY is chained by the neck to the stone wall. A knight of nobility, 30s, with his spirit broken. The door CREAKS open. The Jailor enters, hissing.

> JAILOR
> Sir Oliver Starkey. "Grand" advisor to the Grand
> Master of the Knights of St. John.
>
> (spits in Starkey's face)
> Ya shoulda had the sense to become Protestant
> like the Queen. Stupid Catholic.

And then the Jailor is BASHED on the back of the head from behind. He falls like a sack of dirt at the feet of the two cloaked men. One of them whispers to the unconscious Jailor.

> CLOAKED LEADER
> Stupid Protestant.

They release the surprised Starkey from his chains. Hand him his sword and scabbard.

> CLOAKED LEADER
> There is a boat in the harbor ready to take you
> offshore.

Starkey grasps the man's arm. A pause of gratitude.

INT. DUNGEON CORRIDOR

Two GUARDS walk down the corridor. They see Starkey and the two men, who bolt like rabbits. The Guards pursue.

DOWN ANOTHER CORRIDOR

Starkey and the men stop at a crossroads. The tunnel splits into two. The Guards are gaining.

>   STARKEY
>   Split up!

The two take one corridor, Starkey, the other. The Guards follow the cloaked men.

EXT. ENGLAND PORT - NIGHT

Starkey whisks through the port shadows carrying his broadsword. He looks behind. No one. He stops at a pier.

EXT. ENGLAND LONG PIER

At the end of the pier is a boat loaded with men, waiting for him. He trots toward it. Out of the shadows in front of him steps two ENGLISH GUARDS.

>   GUARD
>   Ho. Where does ye think yer goin'?

Starkey doesn't answer.

>   GUARD
>   Ya looks shady to me.
>   (to the other Guard)
>   Take him.

The Guard goes for him. But Starkey downs him in two swift steps without even drawing his sword. The Lead Guard draws his sword. Starkey still doesn't.

Not far off the pier the two Dungeon Guards appear.

>   DUNGEON GUARD
>   There he is!

The Pier Guard grins with rotting teeth.

DOWN AT THE WAITING BOAT

A knight moves to help Starkey. But he's held back by CAPTAIN ROMEGAS, a fierce and wily Spanish warrior. He gestures the knight to watch and see.

BACK AT THE PIER BATTLE

Starkey dodges each slash of the Guard's sword. He's untouchable. The Guard, frustrated, lunges. Starkey uses his sword, still unsheathed, to whirl and fling the Guard's weapon into the water.

The other Guards reach him. He now draws his sword. The two come at him, swinging like madmen. Starkey casually deflects the blows. He backs up against a set of cannons on the pier.

> STARKEY
> Good God, men. Is that all you've got?

This infuriates the lead Guard. He hauls back and YELLS like an ogre. Swings high and wide. Starkey steps aside. CLANG! The blade crashes on the cannon barrel and snaps in two!

Starkey's blade is at the stunned Guard's throat. A glance to the other, whose sword shakes fearfully in his hands.

> LEAD GUARD
> Go on! Take him, Horace!

But Poor Horace can't. Starkey bolts for the boat. Which is now rowing away! The Sailors yell for him to hurry.

The Lead Guard grabs Horace's sword and takes off after him.

Starkey reaches the end of the pier and leaps over ten feet of water. Lands in the boat with a THUD.

The Lead Guard stops at the end of the pier. No way he can make it. He runs back to the cannons positioned on the pier.

ON THE LEAVING BOAT

Romegas sees the cannons and yells to his oarsmen.

> ROMEGAS
> Faster, lads! Lest we end up cannon fodder!

BACK ON THE PIER

The Guards have a cannon ready. Packing the other one. The first one FIRES. A cannonball hits the water yards from the boat with a huge splash. The sailors row for their lives.

The second cannon is loaded and primed. It FIRES.

ON THE LEAVING BOAT

The second ball hits a few feet away, pitching the boat and drenching the men. Romegas yells back to the pier.

> ROMEGAS
> Good shot!

BACK ON THE PIER

The Guards are angrier than hell, swearing their heads off.

ON THE LEAVING BOAT

Romegas' men cheer and row on, safely out of distance, toward three galleys offshore, barely visible in the dark.

> STARKEY
> Captain Romegas. Thank you for your - help.
> Somewhat reserved though it was.

> ROMEGAS
> At your service, Sir Oliver. You gave quiet a good
> show.

INT. GALLEY HOLD - NIGHT

Starkey writes by candlelight with a quill in his diary. He sways with the back and forth pitch of the ship.

> STARKEY (V.O.)
> April 12, in the year of our Lord, 1565. Leaving my
> beloved England pains me deeply. But political
> expediency -- and the persecution of Catholics by
> Queen Elisabeth --leaves me no choice but to

preserve my life and seek refuge within the
quarters of my own Order...

EXT. GALLEY DECK - DAY

Starkey stands on the deck looking out to sea, his VOICE-OVER continues. Romegas joins him with a mariner's astrolabe, taking navigational readings. They nod to each other.

> STARKEY (V.O.)
> ...Captain Romegas has assured me the Grand
> Master awaits my return to his services with much
> anticipation. Destination: Malta. A tiny
> godforsaken rock of an island. The perfect outpost
> for the last Order of knights left in this
> godforsaken New World.

> ROMEGAS
> Malta is a few days hence. But first, I have some
> business to take care of.

Starkey looks at him, then back out to sea.

> STARKEY (V.O.)
> How long before we too are gone?

EXT. TURKISH MERCHANT SHIP - DAY

> SUPER: MEDITERRANEAN SEA

A Turkish merchant ship guarded by a war galley glides along the shoreline of Africa. The TURKISH CAPTAIN peers through a spyglass. A NAVIGATOR steps up.

> NAVIGATOR
> Captain. By dead reckoning we should arrive in
> Istanbul tomorrow.

> CAPTAIN
> We had better. The Sultan is not patient when it
> comes to his prized possessions.

The Navigator stares at the close shoreline cliff. The Captain looks up. TWO GALLEYS pull out from a hidden cove. On their sails, bright red eight-pointed crosses. Panic hits.

> CAPTAIN
> Christian corsairs. All hands on deck! All hands on deck!

INT. TURKISH MERCHANT SHIP OAR ROOM

Exhausted naked slaves chained in rows strain at oars. A cruel GALLEYMASTER cracks his whip.

> GALLEYMASTER
> Triple speed, Christian swine!

Another crack. The TIMING GONG beats faster, harder.

EXT. TURKISH MERCHANT SHIP DECK

But not fast enough. The Christian galleys are upon them.

> CAPTAIN
> Allah deliver us.

EXT. CHRISTIAN GALLEY

Moments from contact. Romegas stands on the bow dressed in full knight regalia. He barks to his sailors.

> ROMEGAS
> Prepare to board!

Down on deck, knights ready grappling hooks, ropes and planks.

> ROMEGAS
> We will see whose God rules the seas.

RAMMING boats. CRIES of war. Knights mount the Turkish vessel. Starkey swings down on a rope and hits the deck, slashing. Muskets explode. Swords clash. Men fall overboard.

Romegas treads a plank onto the Turk's deck. He walks with purpose, untouched by the surrounding fury. He slices away, dropping Turks left and right without barely a notice. It's like he's unconcerned. And unstoppable.

Starkey is a swashbuckler. He fends off one sailor, sees another, and swaps his sword to his left hand, equally dexterous, agile.

> STARKEY
> Give my regards to the devil!

He runs the Turk through with a fencing ease.

INT. TURKISH MERCHANT SHIP OAR ROOM

The slaves listen to the noise of battle above. Who will win?

The sound of feet trampling down the stairs.

The door opens. The Galley master steps through -- followed at sword point by Romegas! He flings the keys to the slaves.

> ROMEGAS
> Be free, soldiers of the Lord!

CHEERS of victory. The slaves scramble to lose their chains.

EXT. TURKISH MERCHANT SHIP - LATER

Romegas and Starkey stand triumphantly as the defeated Turks are escorted onto the Christian galleys.

A SENIOR KNIGHT approaches with an armful of jewels and gold.

> SENIOR KNIGHT
> Captain Romegas. It appears we have captured
> one of the Sultan's own vessels.

Starkey and Romegas look at each other. A smile spreads across Romegas' face.

> SENIOR KNIGHT
> And there is something else you will want to see.

INT. TURKISH MERCHANT SHIP HOLD

Starkey, Romegas and his sailors fill the passage of the hold. The Senior Knight opens the doorway. Inside, are ten of the most beautiful women in the Muslim world, draped in silken gown and veil, trembling with fear.

> SENIOR KNIGHT
> Some of the Sultan's harem.

Romegas smirks.

> ROMEGAS
> A truly victorious day.

> STARKEY
> Indeed.

> ROMEGAS
> Knights! Do not just stand there, drooling. Carry
> the cargo aboard!

The knights cautiously approach the women.

> ROMEGAS
> You are all captives of the Sovereign Military
> Hospitaller Order of St. John of Jerusalem, of
> Rhodes and of Malta.

The women are escorted out. Starkey locks eyes with a particularly gorgeous one, SELIMA, 20s. She turns away. He watches her leave.

EXT. ESTABLISHING SHOT - ISLAND OF MALTA - DAY

SUPER: ISLE OF MALTA

A small rock of an island. No foliage. Only nine miles long and a few miles wide. Its main harbor, guarded by a CLIFFSIDE FORTRESS and TWO OTHER CASTLES on peninsulas. A threefold defense.

Out in the harbor, a slew of men drag A HUGE CHAIN ten times the size of a ship's anchor onto a series of rafts. It's implanted into the wall of the cliff. Huge guns beside it.

Villager boats drift amongst the galleys of St. John anchored near the shores.

EXT. GRAND HARBOUR PORT, MALTA

The streets are alive with commerce. Merchants, fish markets, foodstuffs. A blacksmith hammers armor into shape.

A small CHILD scurries through the busy village. Up in a window, a maidservant yells, "Gardey loo!" and pours a chamber pot onto the street. The child dodges. The splash hits a villager.

The child reaches a squad of knights in conversation. He tugs at one of their red cloaks, decorated with the white eight-pointed cross of St. John.

> KNIGHT
> Child! Begone! We are conversing with the Grand
> Master!

The knights halt. They part. Out steps LA VALETTE, 70-years old and decked in the ornamental armor of a Grand Master. A man with the courage of a hundred warriors and the compassion of a priest. A perfect mixture of justice and mercy.

He bends down. A smile brings comfort and the boy points to the pier. Romegas' galleys arrive towing the Turkish ships.

> LA VALETTE
> Suffer the little children, brothers. You may learn a
> thing or two from them.

The knights look at each other like scolded children.

EXT. GRAND HARBOUR PIER - DAY

Romegas jumps down off his ship, followed by knights carrying trunks loaded with the Sultan's treasures. The crowd parts for La Valette and his men. Romegas kneels before La Valette.

> ROMEGAS
> Grand Master La Valette. I present to you
> treasures captured from a galley of Turkish royal
> Sultan Suleiman...
>> (sarcastically)
> ...the Magnificent.

> LA VALETTE
> Well done, Commander Romegas.

Starkey steps off the boat. La Valette sees him. Starkey walks proudly up to him and kneels.

> STARKEY
> Grand Master.

La Valette pulls him up.

> LA VALETTE
>
> Sir Oliver. My Secretary of War. I have missed
> you.

> STARKEY
>
> Begging your pardon, sir. I was a trifle delayed by
> the Queen.

La Valette grins. Hugs him fiercely. The crowd HUSHES. Everyone turns. The harem women are escorted off the boat. Mouths drop with awe. La Valette and Starkey notice.

> STARKEY
>
> It appears our spoils may prove a bit of a
> temptation for the Order.

> LA VALETTE
>
> Sir Oliver, your wit notwithstanding, recall your
> vows.

> STARKEY
>
> Poverty, chastity and obedience. How can I forget?

> LA VALETTE
>
> I expect all of the brethren to have as unfailing
> memory as your own.

Starkey smirks. The harem stands before La Valette.

> LA VALETTE
> (to Romegas)
> Quarter them in the English Hospice.
> (glancing at Starkey)
> And post a guard.

> ROMEGAS
>
> Yes, Grand Master.

Romegas guides the harem away.

INT. GRAND MASTER'S LODGE, MALTA - DAY

La Valette poses valiantly in his armor for a PAINTER painting his portrait. Starkey stands nearby, watching. He is a shrewd political advisor.

LA VALETTE
Your travels abroad have made you cynical,
Secretary.

STARKEY
Realistic, sir. Time to think in prison.

LA VALETTE
Persecution should strengthen virtue.

STARKEY
The knighthood is no longer a virtuous
pilgrimage. It has become a haven of mercenaries.

LA VALETTE
King Henry dissolved the Order in England years
ago. You alone remained. This, because you are a
mercenary?
(no reply from Starkey)
Chivalry is not dead, Sir Oliver. We are foremost,
a holy order.

STARKEY
Means to an end, sir.

La Valette gives him a dirty look.

STARKEY
The fact is, "a virtuous man necessarily comes to
grief among so many who are not virtuous."

LA VALETTE
You read too much Machiavelli.

STARKEY
The world is changing. And no one can stop it.
Renaissance in Florence. Reformation in Germany.

LA VALETTE
That infernal monk, Luther.

> STARKEY
>
> On the outside, the common soldier is obedient.
> But away from your presence, he is true only to
> himself.

This bothers La Valette. He gives a look of disbelief.

> STARKEY
>
> I can prove it.

> LA VALETTE
>
> How so?

> STARKEY
>
> Anonymity.

La Valette looks puzzled. Starkey smiles deviously.

EXT. MALTA STREETS - NIGHT

La Valette and Starkey walk along the street in common monk's robes. They pull their hoods over their faces.

> STARKEY
>
> Prepare yourself for the scalding reality of knights
> freed from the presence of their Grand Master.

INT. MALTA TAVERN - NIGHT

The tap is flowing. MINSTRELS sing an Arthurian tale with hornpipe, flute and tabor.

At a table in the corner, three obnoxious knights gamble with dice and drink ale. Whores in their arms: An arrogant FRENCH Bailiff, a temperamental SCOT, and a bitter GERMAN with too many scars on his face.

> SCOT
>
> Did ye gander the look of fancy on the Grand
> Master's face when those harem wenches strutted
> about?

> GERMAN
>
> I think he is saving them for himself.

SCOT

Do ya think he can still get it up?

They all LAUGH. The Frenchman only smirks.

Over by the bar, disguised monks, La Valette and Starkey, hear it all. La Valette is pierced by the brazenness.

FRENCHMAN

It is not his cock I'm worried about. More his ability to lead in battle.

SCOT

How old is the bastard?

FRENCHMAN

Seventy, and then some.

SCOT

That makes two things he cannot get up. His cock and his broadsword!

More LAUGHS. La Valette starts for them. Starkey holds him back. La Valette storms out. Starkey follows.

EXT. MALTA TAVERN - NIGHT

Outside, church bells RING. A NIGHTWATCHMAN with candle lantern BARKS curfew. La Valette stands away from the door, disturbed by what he has seen.

LA VALETTE

Gamblers. Whoremongers. Drunkards.

STARKEY

But they are still excellent soldiers.

LA VALETTE

Sir Oliver. Virtue is the highest mark of excellence.

STARKEY

It is a new world, m'lord. Virtue has given way to utility.

LA VALETTE

Utility without virtue can only lead to evil.

A couple knights pass by, roaring with bawdy LAUGHTER. One BELCHES like a horse. La Valette and Starkey pull back.

INT. MALTA TAVERN - NIGHT

Back to the obnoxious knights. The German glances at a harlot by his side. He grabs a bite of pig feet. Leans in and mutters.

> GERMAN
> I say we bag those pagan harem wenches and
> feast on some illicit meat!

The men stop in thought. The harlots frown.

> FRENCHMAN
> We are entitled to the spoils of war.

They glance at one another.

EXT. MALTA TAVERN - NIGHT

The knights bustle out of the tavern and are startled by the two monks. They hide their guilt.

> FRENCHMAN
> Brothers.

La Valette doesn't respond. So Starkey does.

> STARKEY
> Brothers.

The knights walk guiltily off into darkness. La Valette moves to follow. Starkey sighs but accompanies his Grand Master.

INT. ENGLISH HOSPICE, HAREM QUARTERS - NIGHT

The harem women relax in their housing. Beautiful Selima looks out the window in longing. Below her, TWO KNIGHTS guard the entrance to the Hospice. She closes the window.

EXT. ENGLISH HOSPICE - NIGHT

Down below, the Frenchman walks by the guards. The guards straighten and salute the Bailiff. They watch the Frenchman pass. The German and Scot slip up behind them, swing clubs and drop the guards. They drag the guards into the building.

INT. ENGLISH HOSPICE, HAREM QUARTERS - NIGHT

The door opens. The harem women turn. In walk the three rogues. The German loosens his crotch panel.

Selima, unafraid, stands up. Another WOMAN rises, hoping to avert disaster. The German smacks the woman hard. Seizes her. Harem SCREAM. The other men grab for sport.

The Scot throws Selima to the floor. Cracks her. Pins her violently. She flails. He smacks her again.

EXT. ENGLISH HOSPICE

La Valette and Starkey arrive at the unguarded post. La Valette opens the door. Inside, the two guards, out like lights. Faint SCREAMS above.

> STARKEY
> Sir! Announce your presence!

La Valette stops him. Shakes his head no.

INT. ENGLISH HOSPICE

The women are ravaged by the beasts. The Scot slobbers over Selima, her gown ripped open, trying to hold her still to have his way.

The doors crash open. Two mad monks, robes flowing. The knights stop and look at each other.

> FRENCHMAN
> It looks like we caught the molesters, gentlemen.

The knights draw weapons.

Starkey gives La Valette a look to reveal himself. La Valette shakes his head no. Starkey rolls his eyes. They pull swords from beneath their robes. Surprise.

Sword fight. Starkey sees Selima and moves for the Scot

La Valette takes on the German and Frenchman.

The Scot's temper makes him sloppy. Starkey skewers him to the wall.

> STARKEY
>
> That will teach you to keep your codpiece closed.

Starkey's sword is stuck, so he takes the Scot's blade.

> STARKEY
>
> May I borrow this? Thank you.

La Valette adds another scar to the German's face. He HOWLS in pain. Holds his eye in his hands. The Frenchman runs.

Starkey tends to Selima. The Frenchman surprises him with a swipe to his side. He stumbles back, wounded.

The Frenchman grabs Selima and holds a pistol to her temple. La Valette and Starkey freeze.

> FRENCHMAN
>
> Drop the swords, brothers. Except ye have no
> concern for innocent life.

> LA VALETTE
>
> You -- are not my brother.

> FRENCHMAN
>
> Drop them!

La Valette's sword drops. Starkey follows his lead. The Frenchman smiles. Aims the pistol at La Valette, ready to fire. But La Valette pulls down his hood. Shock. The pistol tremors. The Frenchman drops to his knees.

> FRENCHMAN
>
> Lord Grand Master.

La Valette raises his sword in vengeance. But his conscience halts him. His sword lowers.

> LA VALETTE
>
> Sir Oliver. Place this man under arrest.
>   (he sees Starkey's bloody side)
> And get yourself to the Infirmary.

Starkey holds his wounded side and picks up the pistol to lead the Frenchman away. La Valette bends down to Selima to see her wounds. She's bruised and bloody.

LA VALETTE
Perhaps it is a new world.

Selima looks away, avoids eye contact.

EXT. MALTA JAIL - NIGHT

Starkey exits the jail and limps down the street, blood leaking through his clothes. Before him, the Sacred Infirmary. His head spins. He blacks out.

INT. SACRED INFIRMARY WARD, MALTA - NIGHT

Starkey comes to in the long Infirmary ward lined with beds. Before him is La Valette, dressed in orderly garb and tending to the Secretary himself. Starkey tries to get up but is calmed by his superior.

STARKEY
Please, sir. I am unworthy of your service.

LA VALETTE
Nonsense. We are Hospitallers. "Serf and slave to our lords, the sick." Now, I will have no more resistance from you. Is that clear?

Starkey quiets down. He looks over and sees a stretcher carried past him. It's Selima! Their eyes connect.

STARKEY
Yes sir. I will content myself to stay as long as possible.

La Valette is surprised by the sudden turn. Starkey looks over to the hallway where Selima was.

INT. SULTAN SULEIMAN'S PALACE, - DAY

SUPER: ISTANBUL, TURKEY

Frenzied belly dancers. A CACOPHONY of Oriental music. Rich foods presented before Turkish nobility. At the head of the feast is SULTAN SULEIMAN the Magnificent. 70 years of conquering wisdom. The wisest ruler of Islam. But a man with thin patience.

A MESSENGER approaches. Whispers to him. The Sultan signals a trumpeter, who blows his horn and the party's over.

> TRUMPETER
> The military counsel will convene!

INT. SULEIMAN'S WAR ROOM - DAY

Suleiman's advisors sit on embroidered carpets, arguing. In the middle, a large map of the Mediterranean.

There are three here to remember: DRAGUT, late 60s, military genius. Suleiman alone does not pale in this titan's presence.

General MUSTAPHA, younger, jealous of Dragut. A warmonger.

PIALI, Mustapha's rival, is a sly political fox. A man you cannot trust.

They all quiet down as the large doors open and an obnoxiously nasal HERALD announces to rolling drums.

> HERALD
> Sultan Suleiman the Magnificent of the Ottomans,
> Majestic Caesar, Royal Emperor, Prince of
> Nations, Ruler of the Faithful, Possessor of men's
> necks, King of kings and Lord of lords, Allah's
> general dispensing peace on earth and good will
> toward all men! Allah be praised!

The advisors prostrate themselves. Suleiman walks in, his favored wife, ROXELANA, by his side. He is annoyed.

> SULEIMAN
> Up! Up!

They get up and he sits among them, angrily brushing away a servant with waving palm branch.

> SULEIMAN
> What is this insolence that reaches my ears?

The council is sheepish. Mustapha spills the news.

> MUSTAPHA
> Your royal highness, it appears Christian corsairs
> have captured a vessel of the court. Laden with
> valuables.

PIALI
Eighty thousand ducats.

ROXELANA
And some of your harem!

SULEIMAN
(annoyed)
Roxelana.

Roxelana pulls back, reluctantly submissive.

SULEIMAN
Hospitallers?

Mustapha and Piali nod heads. Not what he wanted to hear.

SULEIMAN
(to himself)
La Valette.

Dragut silently knows the Sultan's displeasure. Mustapha is unaware.

MUSTAPHA
Sire, these infidels must be destroyed!

Suleiman peers at Mustapha. He's out of line.

PIALI
Your majesty, beg patience for Mustapha. His
betrothed was on the ship. Love can aggravate the
emotions.

This jab perturbs Mustapha. Suleiman smiles at him.

SULEIMAN
Finally, one of my court understands my own
disposition.

Suleiman glances slyly at an agitated Roxelana.

Mustapha reacts vindicated and Piali tries to recover ground.

                    PIALI
Your highness. So long as Malta remains in the
hands of the knights, your empire remains
divided. Their piracy threatens passage by sea.

                    MUSTAPHA
If you do not take the island, all communications
between Africa and Istanbul will eventually be
blocked.

                    SULEIMAN
That cursed rock is an obstruction in my anal
cavity.

The advisors try to hold back their chuckles.

                    SULEIMAN
I should never have let those sons of Satan free at
Rhodes.

                    PIALI
That was forty years ago, your highness. The isle
of Rhodes remains your glory. Malta can be as
well.

Suleiman has trouble trusting his sycophants.

                    SULEIMAN
What say you, Dragut?

Dragut finally speaks. And when he does, everyone listens.

                    DRAGUT
Most holy sire. I advise against it.

                    SULEIMAN
Why?

                    DRAGUT
Malta is not Rhodes. It is distant, barren.
Communications and supplies difficult to
maintain.

MUSTAPHA
We can seize that puny little island in a fortnight!

Dragut glares at Mustapha, who looks to Suleiman for support.

DRAGUT
And there is one more thing. -- This La Valette and
his knights of St. John. They are desperate
warriors who fight to the death.

SULEIMAN
The mighty Dragut speaks from experience?

DRAGUT
The Sultan must prepare for the loss of many
faithful subjects to obtain so useless a possession.

SULEIMAN
(sarcastic)
Oh, wise and cautious Dragut.

Dragut bows discreetly. It's made him great.

Suleiman looks at the big map.

SULEIMAN
There is growing civilization in Europe.

MUSTAPHA
And much division, my lord.

PIALI
The Christians are at war with one another.

Everyone agrees. Roxelana leans in to Suleiman.

ROXELANA
There are many riches in Rome. -- And beautiful
women.

Suleiman considers.

SULEIMAN
Dragut. Would Malta be a sufficient encampment
from which to invade the Christian empire?

Dragut nods reluctantly.

> PIALI
> A plan of unfaltering wisdom, sire. Your greatness
> is once again unapproachable.

> SULEIMAN
> Shut up, Piali.

Piali withdraws, humiliated. Dragut smirks.

Suleiman considers the importance of his decision in an uncomfortable silence.
Then, finally...

> SULEIMAN
> My desire is a full scale assault on the island of
> Malta.
>> (beat)
> Admiral Piali will lead the sea forces.

Piali glimmers with pride.

> SULEIMAN
> Commander Mustapha, the land forces.

Piali drops. Mustapha gloats.

> SULEIMAN
> And Dragut will arrive later as overseer.

Now Piali, Mustapha and Dragut all look disappointed.

> SULEIMAN
> No move will be made apart from Dragut's
> advice.

> PIALI
> But your highness...

> MUSTAPHA
> Three commanders?

> SULEIMAN
> The Sultan has decreed. Let Allah's will be done.
> Allah be praised.

EVERYONE
Allah be praised.

SULEIMAN
Let us be done with this gadfly La Valette and his
pestering Knights of St. John.

Suleiman rams a knife into the map island of Malta.

SULEIMAN
There can only be one Emperor on earth. One God
in heaven.

Dragut stares at the knife and map in a trance.

INT. SULEIMAN'S WAR ROOM HALLWAY - DAY

The doors burst open and Suleiman exits with his entourage. A nervous
ATTENDANT looks around. Slips out the back.

INT. SERVANT'S ROOM, SULEIMAN'S PALACE

The Attendant sits at a table with quill and paper. He squeezes a lemon into a
small cup and uses the juice as invisible ink to write between the lines of a bill of
sale. He is a SPY.

A NOISE outside the door startles him. It's nothing. He places the bill into an
envelope.

EXT. PORT OF ISTANBUL, TURKEY - NIGHT

The port is rife with preparations for war. Galleys are loaded with supplies.
Turkish soldiers march the streets.

The Attendant Spy sneaks past a posted guard and over to a merchant ship tied
to the pier.

He meets a sailor in the shadows. Hands him the envelope. The sailor slips up
the plank and onto the merchant vessel.

INT. GRAND MASTER'S PALACE, MALTA - NIGHT

A long wooden table. Walls plastered with paintings of Hospitaller heroes. La
Valette sits before an irate mob of Maltese locals CHATTERING with discontent.

He can't hear a thing. Romegas approaches. La Valette turns to the crowd like a chastising father.

> LA VALETTE
>
> Please - be - silent!

Everyone shuts up in an instant. Romegas leans in. Whispers.

> ROMEGAS
>
> Dispatch from our spies in Istanbul, sir.

La Valette is concerned.

> LA VALETTE
>
> Decipher it and report back to me.

Romegas salutes and leaves. La Valette turns to the crowd.

> LA VALETTE
>
> Now, please. Not all at once.

The MAYOR, a funny little man trying to please all sides, steps forward.

> MAYOR
>
> Lord Grand Master, ruler of the Hospitallers...

> LA VALETTE
>
> Spare the formalities, Mayor.

> MAYOR
> (clears his throat)
> Well. Evidently, that is, some say, that, well, the
> Order continues to, shall we say, take advantage
> of their status on the island.

> PEASANT
>
> I'd call it pillage and plunder!

The crowd grumbles restlessly. A NOBLEMAN speaks out.

> NOBLEMAN
>
> For forty years, these so-called, "Knights of
> Justice" have been flaunting their nobility on the
> island and attempting to disabuse us of our own!

The crowd murmurs again. La Valette sits patiently, a father with his children. The tavern Innkeeper steps up.

> INNKEEPER
> And they are constantly engaged in brawls.
> Fighting, destroying property. They have no
> chivalry, sire.

> PEASANT
> Where's our justice?!

The crowd rises to a new height of dissatisfaction.

INT. GRAND MASTER'S PALACE, SIDE ROOM

Romegas holds the dispatch over a candle. Heat catalyzes the hidden lemon juice. Secret handwriting materializes.

INT. GRAND MASTER'S PALACE

La Valette calms the restless herd. His countenance is heavy.

> LA VALETTE
> My dear Maltese. I assume full responsibility for
> the disorderly conduct of my men. Please accept
> my deepest apologies...

The crowd hushes in respect at such a truly good man.

Romegas enters, halting La Valette. He holds the dispatch. Whispers to La Valette. Dread sweeps over the mighty leader.

INT. SACRED INFIRMARY WARD, MALTA - DAY

Starkey is awake in his bed. He looks up. The orderlies are out. The way is clear. He slips out of bed and into the adjoining hallway.

INT. SACRED INFIRMARY, MUSLIM WARD

In a side room, Selima rests in her bed. She hears a sound. Re-veils her face. In limps Starkey.

She utters a word in Turkish. He doesn't understand. Language barrier. He sighs to himself.

> STARKEY
> Beautiful sweet maiden.

And then out of nowhere...

> SELIMA
> Thank you.

Starkey's eyes explode in shock. She can speak English! Embarrassed, he doesn't know what to do. So, he stumbles back out the door, right smack into an Orderly in the hall.

> ORDERLY
> The Grand Master has called a Chapter General.

Without a second's delay, Starkey is off and limping.

> ORDERLY
> But, sir! You are not supposed to leave the
> Infirmary!

BACK IN SELIMA'S ROOM

Selima looks out the door. Beside her, a curtain pulls aside, and a harem woman giggles. Selima whips the curtain back. Pulls out a small Koran from within her dress.

The Orderly is there. He sees the Koran. Snatches it up.

> ORDERLY
> Idol worshipper.

Selima averts her gaze in servility. But in her eyes, anger.

INT. CHAPTER GENERAL HOUSE, MALTA - DAY

Starkey stumbles through the doors of the Chapter General. The hall is filled with Knights. At the front, La Valette. Next to him, Romegas.

> LA VALETTE
> Knights Hospitaller. We have had forty years of
> relative obscurity with which to perform our duty
> to the poor and the infirm. But the pagan emperor,
> Sultan Suleiman, has seen fit to extend his
> malignant rule further into Christendom.

The knights get uneasy.

>   LA VALETTE
>   Our spies have confirmed that this Infidel is
>   planning an all-out assault on our blessed island
>   of Malta.

The knights go still. Starkey stiffens in shock.

>   LA VALETTE
>   I have sent a call to all knights in Europe to their
>   duty by our side. I have sent word to King Philip
>   of Spain requesting twenty-five thousand
>   reinforcements.

Complete silence fills the hall. One knight leans to another.

>   KNIGHT
>   My God. How many of them are there?

La Valette remains undeterred.

>   LA VALETTE
>   Well, what are you waiting for, soldiers? Prepare
>   for war!

And the hall erupts with a thunderous cheer. Starkey is filled with dread.

MONTAGE OF PREPARATIONS FOR WAR AT THREE FORTS OF MALTA:

EXT. ST. ELMO'S FORTRESS, MALTA - DAY

The five-pointed star fortress of St. Elmo rests on a cliff overlooking the harbor. Slaves haul stone to reinforce the RAVELIN, a second wall fifty yards outside the actual walls of the castle, creating a double barricade of protection.

At the cliff's edge, a contingent of ARQUEBUSIERS (musket-like marksmen) ready their rifles. A soldier slings a large rock in the air. It explodes under a volley of fire.

EXT. FORT BIRGU, MALTA - DAY

In the second fort across the harbor, more slaves break their backs reinforcing and widening the castle walls of Birgu.

EXT. FORT SENGLEA, MALTA - DAY

Next to the peninsula of Birgu is the third stronghold on its own peninsula: Senglea. In Senglea's yard, knights line up in sword practice, helped by SQUIRES. La Valette watches with pride.

But there are also the local Maltese militia, being trained by knights in tactical defense. They are a proud people unwilling to let the knights have all the glory.

Glaring in the wings, are the Maltese Nobles, watching it all bitterly, unwilling to participate.

INT. THE COURT OF KING PHILIP, SPAIN - DAY

SUPER: MADRID, SPAIN

SALVAGO, faithful messenger of La Valette, and DON GARCIA DE TOLEDO, Admiral of the Spanish fleet, kneel before the throne of the impetuous self-absorbed KING PHILIP II. He is a ruler with but one thing on his mind: family dynasty.

> KING PHILIP
> Absolutely not. I will not hear of it.

> DON GARCIA
> But your majesty, I know the man. La Valette is proud. He would never send request unless he was truly in need.

> KING PHILIP
> I do not care.

Don Garcia looks at Salvago hopelessly.

> KING PHILIP
> I will not send those kinds of numbers for the defense of a lifeless rock. I need my soldiers in Spain.

> DON GARCIA
> Your majesty. If you please. It may seem an insignificant island, but it is the key to Europe. If Suleiman takes Malta, he will be hours from Sicily. Days from Spain.

KING PHILIP
My dear viceroy. If your navy is weakened at
Malta, who will then protect Spain and Sicily from
their advance?

Finally, Salvago speaks up.

SALVAGO
Your highness. If Don Garcia's galleys do not give
aid to Malta, it will no longer matter.

Philip pauses in circumspection. A point well made.

EXT. ISTANBUL HARBOR, TURKEY - DAY

200 Turkish war galleys crowd the harbor of the Golden Horn awaiting their
command. Suleiman sits in his portable throne looking out on his mighty
armada. About him, a festival of dancing and celebration. Piali and Mustapha
stand before him in their Ottoman regalia. Dragut, skeptical, restrained.
Suleiman raises his arm and the harbor goes silent.

SULEIMAN
Behold! This day, the mighty arm of Allah sets
forth to crush the infidel!

The mob erupts in worship and praise. He lowers his arm.

EXT. TURKISH GALLEY DECK

Sailors hoist their anchors with a heave ho.

INT. TURKISH GALLEY, OAR ROOM

Pacers beat their timing gongs. Galley masters crack their whips. Slaves strain at
the oars.

EXT. ISTANBUL HARBOR

Galleys leave the harbor in quest of war. Suleiman turns to Dragut.

SULEIMAN
What say you now, Dragut?

>   DRAGUT
>   (sarcastic)
>   A magnificent spectacle, your royal highness.
>   Surely, Allah himself is mightily impressed.

Suleiman rolls his eyes at the sarcasm.

INT. SACRED INFIRMARY WARD, MALTA - DAY

Starkey has his bandage changed. He's stronger, now. In the shadow of the hallway, Selima watches him.

EXT. MALTA CROP FIELD - DAY

Just outside the cities, Maltese take torches to their fields of wheat, burning them to the ground. Making the already barren landscape even more uninhabitable.

EXT. MALTA VILLAGE - DAY

Village families and their animals are herded into the fortresses, leaving surrounding towns empty.

EXT. SACRED INFIRMARY ROOF - DAY

Selima stands on the roof of the Infirmary watching the preparations. Billows of black smoke ascend from the fields on the horizon.

Selima senses a presence. Over by the door, Starkey. She averts her look. He approaches her. She tries to leave, but he grabs her. She panics. Struggles. Starkey releases her.

>   STARKEY
>   You think I am to hurt you?

She looks away. Then he understands.

>   STARKEY
>   I am heathen to you.
>
>   (beat, amused)
>   And what do you think you are to me?

Selima finally looks at him.

SELIMA

Then why do you approach me with such deliberation?

STARKEY
(smiles)
Actually, I am a bit more broad-minded than my fellow monks.
(beat)
What is your name?

SELIMA

Selima.

STARKEY

Well, Selima, I am Sir Oliver Starkey. And you rather startled me earlier with your knowledge of the English tongue. Where did you learn?

SELIMA

I was captured from Christian parents and raised in the Sultan's palace.

He looks even more interested.

SELIMA

Perhaps I am not as heathen as you suspect.

STARKEY

Perhaps you will return to the faith of your father.

SELIMA

Perhaps you will submit to Allah.

Starkey backs down.

STARKEY

Are you as bold before your Sultan?

SELIMA

I have never seen the Sultan.

This shocks him.

> SELIMA

Some of us never will. Europeans think the
seraglio is a nightly orgy of the Sultan's
indulgence. But his favorite, Roxelana, is a jealous
wife. She keeps the Sultan busy -- and the harem
out of sight.

> STARKEY

Well, the Sultan is at loss, then.

Selima stares out into the landscape.

> SELIMA

I am not of the harem.

This interests Starkey. He brightens.

> SELIMA

I belong to another. Mustapha Pasha. Leader of
the Sultan's land forces.

> STARKEY

Well this is news. The wife of a General?

> SELIMA

I am betrothed. Not wed.

> STARKEY

Do you love him?

> SELIMA

Love is not a luxury afforded to me.

Starkey moves closer with a hopeful look.

> STARKEY

Perhaps it can be. You are in a different world
now.

She pulls back.

> SELIMA

I do not consider my circumstances much
changed.

Starkey smiles, impressed with her bravado.

> STARKEY
> I have not seen your face.

He slowly reaches up to her veil. But she pulls back and walks briskly away. He watches her hungrily.

INT. SACRED INFIRMARY, STARKEY'S BED - DAY

Starkey packs his few belongings at his bedside. He turns. Selima is behind him. He returns to his packing.

> SELIMA
> Please forgive my lack of charity.

He pauses. Then continues.

> SELIMA
> I have been allowed to nurse the wounded.

> STARKEY
> I am released from the Infirmary.
>   (slyly)
> God willing, I will be injured again.

He turns back to her. Looks into her eyes. She reaches up and drops her veil from her face.

She is a goddess.

The sound of an Orderly rolling a cart startles her. She quickly re-veils and whisks away. Starkey smiles to himself.

INT. LA VALETTE'S WAR ROOM

La Valette stands over a map of the Grand Harbor with Romegas and other senior officers. Starkey enters.

> STARKEY
> Grand Master.

> LA VALETTE
> You are in cheerful spirits, Sir Oliver. The
> infirmary revived your body?

> STARKEY
> (smiling broadly)
> And my soul, sir.

Starkey joins them. La Valette points to the map.

> LA VALETTE
> If the Turks land on the north side of the island,
> they will take the capital, Mdina. We have not
> enough men to protect that city. We will
> concentrate upon the Harbor forts. St. Elmo, Birgu,
> and Senglea. And pray they land on the southern
> tip.

> ROMEGAS
> With Don Garcia's reinforcements, we should
> have a fighting chance, sir.

> LA VALETTE
> Even so. God help us.

They are interrupted by a messenger.

> MESSENGER
> Grand Master! Don Garcia has arrived!

EXT. GRAND HARBOUR PORT, MALTA - DAY

Six galleys docked at port. La Valette steps up with Starkey, Romegas and a reception of officers. Don Garcia approaches with his entourage and bows.

> DON GARCIA
> Grand Master La Valette. Don Garcia de Toledo,
> Viceroy of Sicily, at your service.

Next to him is COPIER, a rugged veteran of guerrilla warfare.

> DON GARCIA
> Grand Marshal Copier and his cavalry.

Copier bows. La Valette acknowledges.

Don Garcia waves forward a group of Scotsmen, led by handsome, sharp JAMES SANDILANDS.

DON GARCIA
Sir James Sandilands, master of incendiary
weapons.

Sandilands kneels. La Valette nods. Turns to Don Garcia.

LA VALETTE
Where are the rest of the soldiers?

DON GARCIA
I have a thousand. Gunners, Spanish troops and
forty knights from about Europe.

Starkey rolls his eyes at Don Garcia's thick-headedness.

LA VALETTE
That means I now have six hundred knights and a
few thousand soldiers with which to hold off the
entire Ottoman fleet?

Don Garcia gropes for something. Anything.

DON GARCIA
This is but the first installment. I am preparing
twenty-five thousand men for my return --upon
final approval of the king.

STARKEY
(disheartened)
Upon final approval of the king.

LA VALETTE
Does good king Philip realize the ramifications of
this battle?

DON GARCIA
The king has many concerns.

STARKEY
The Inquisition being one of them.

LA VALETTE
Let us hope they include the future of
Christendom. Please advise the king if we do not

receive reinforcements, I do not know how long
we can hold out before every man is slaughtered.

Sandilands and Copier look at each other. La Valette turns and tramps away. Everyone follows him but Starkey, who stares contemptuously at the humiliated Don Garcia.

EXT. MALTA SHORELINE - DAY

A seagull glides lazily up above. From out of nowhere, a FALCON dives and snatches the bird right out of the sky.

Starkey and La Valette are on the crest of a hill with their horses watching the predator falcon carry its prey. La Valette holds his arm outstretched with falconer's glove. The Falcon homes in and lands gracefully on his human mount.

Copier and his cavalry approach them on horseback.

> COPIER
> Grand Master, the locals know this island like the
> back of their hand. Just let these Turkish bastards
> try to land anywhere. We will make them scurry
> back to the sea like the scavengers they are.

La Valette smiles. Copier yells to his men and they ride on.

> STARKEY
> Guerrilla forces are no match for sheer numbers.

> LA VALETTE
> Have a little courage, Secretary.

> STARKEY
> Strategy is of more concern to me than heroism,
> my lord.

> LA VALETTE
> Promoting "lack of virtue" again?

> STARKEY
> Better a live rat than a dead lion.

LA VALETTE
And that, my dear Starkey, is why you understand
not what real freedom is.

Starkey looks away, bothered.

INT. CASTLE WALLS, MALTA - DAY

Sandilands and his men mix pitch, salt petre, turpentine and resin in big vats.
They fill up small clay pots with the combustibles and close them off with wicks
on the top. Hand grenades. Large copper tubes called "trumps" are piled up.
Large hoops are soaked in the vats of chemicals. All of this will come in use later
during battle.

INT. BLACKSMITH'S FORGE - NIGHT

Blacksmiths work through the night non-stop, beating out armor and weapons.
Sweat mixes with steel and smoke.

Firearms are cleaned. Barrels of gunpowder rolled into place.

EXT. GRAND HARBOR BAY SHORELINE - DAY

Starkey walks Selima along the shoreline.

In the background, the huge chain that crosses the harbor.

SELIMA
The Sultan's army is on its way to Malta.

He can't respond. He stops her.

STARKEY
Selima. I want to tell you something.

He looks deep into her eyes. Before he can, she turns away.

SELIMA
We two follow different Gods.

STARKEY
Are they really all that different?

SELIMA
"Thou shalt have no gods before me."

> STARKEY

The world is changing, Selima. I am losing faith in the intolerance of religion.

> SELIMA

I do not understand.

Starkey looks at her, wondering how to explain it all to her.

> STARKEY

King Henry dissolved the English Langue of my Order when he broke from the Church. I refused to obey. I was vowed a knight of Malta, I would remain a knight of Malta. By the time Elisabeth took the throne, I alone was left. And I went proudly to jail ready to face the chopping block for my "vows." It was the same dungeon cell where only a few years earlier, I had helped incarcerate Protestants. I am beginning to wonder just what "God" I am vowed to after all.

> SELIMA

M'lord. I am a captive and a slave. You are an aristocrat preparing for war. If the Sultan conquers your island, I will be liberated, and you will be enslaved.

> STARKEY

And if the Sultan is thwarted?

She looks at him. They both know he is wrong.

EXT. GRAND HARBOUR PORT

Soldiers float the rafts carrying the huge chain across the harbor. It's attached to another mount and is pulled taught. It spans the entire harbor, blocking any ship from entering. And cannons guard the mounts.

INT. ST. ELMO TOWER, MALTA - DAY

Up in the tower, watchmen play dice. One of them scans the sea through an eyepiece. Miles of expanse. And then he sees it. Horror sweeps over him. 200

Turkish war galleys break the horizon with the portent of disaster. He drops the eyepiece with a YELP and runs down the stairs. One of the other watchmen picks up the eyepiece and looks out. He sees the fleet of doom approaching.

> WATCHMAN
> Mother of God deliver us.

Church bells TOLL in a frenzy throughout the island.

EXTREME CLOSE-UP SHOTS OF TWO KNIGHTS BEING ARMORED:

Jackets of chainmail are pulled over torsos.

Metal spurs are pulled over feet.

SQUIRES buckle on breastplates and backs.

Hands thrust into steel gauntlets.

Glorious gilded swords are sheathed in their scabbards.

Helmets pulled over heads. Visors thrown back.

The knights are La Valette and Starkey. Grand Master in golden ornamental armor and his Secretary of War.

INT. ST. CHRISTOPHER'S CHAPEL, MALTA - DAY

A hundred commanding knights armed to the teeth fill the chapel of St. Christopher.

Starkey is up front with La Valette. A hush goes over the troops.

> LA VALETTE
> Knights of St. John. I have special dispatch from
> Rome. Pope Pius has granted us plenary
> indulgences. All sins are forgiven in light of the
> battle we are about to engage in with the infidel.

> KNIGHT IN THE CROWD
> Thank God!

Knights CHUCKLE nervously. Sandilands frowns and looks away. Up front, A PRIEST holds the wafer and cup.

> PRIEST
> Receive now the holy Eucharist. The body and
> blood of our Lord, Jesus Christ.

La Valette kneels and receives the transubstantiated host. The knights line up in procession.

But not Sandilands and his men. They don't leave their pews.

Starkey and La Valette notice.

So does the devious scandal-mongering Inquisitor, IGNATIUS, who sits on his royal chair.

EXT. OTTOMAN FLAGSHIP AT SEA - DAY

Mustapha perched atop the bow, inspires his soldiers.

> MUSTAPHA
> Mighty warriors of Islam! We are about to land on
> the southern tip of the island. We will not
> encounter opposition until we besiege the castles
> in the harbor. And when we do, Paradise and a
> harem of virgins await any soldier who dies in
> battle for Allah!

The warriors CHEER.

> SOLDIERS
> Jihad! Jihad! Jihad!

INT. INQUISITOR'S PALACE, MALTA - DAY

Sandilands and his two men are under guard before a disturbed La Valette and Starkey and the bloodthirsty Ignatius.

> IGNATIUS
> Unacceptable! You stand before the offices of the
> Holy Inquisition!

Sandilands doesn't dignify Ignatius with acknowledgement of his presence. He speaks to La Valette alone.

> SANDILANDS
> We are innocent of any crime, Grand Master.

LA VALETTE
You refused the host. That is a sign of heresy.

Sandilands' men look at him for response. He sighs. A messenger enters carrying a pamphlet. He hands it to Ignatius. An evil grin spreads across his face.

IGNATIUS
So now it all comes clear. Luther's Ninety-Five
Theses.

Ignatius hands the pamphlet to a thunderstruck La Valette.

IGNATIUS
This book was found in your belongings, Sir
Sandilands. Index Librorum Prohibitorum.

STARKEY
(under his breath)
Forbidden books.

IGNATIUS
It appears we have some Protestant apostates
within our ranks.

SANDILANDS
Grand Master. We are loyal to the Order and to
you.

IGNATIUS
Enough! Put these heretics to the Question.

La Valette knows the score. There's nothing he can do.

The Scotsmen flood with fear. The guards take them away. Ignatius is delirious with pleasure.

IGNATIUS
This Protestant heresy is a stubborn faith. Perhaps
we can purge them of it.

EXT. MALTA SOUTHERN SHORELINE - NIGHT

Landing parties of Turkish soldiers quietly slip ashore.

INT. MUSTAPHA'S COMMANDER'S TENT

Mustapha and Piali quarrel over a map of the island.

> PIALI
>
> Mustapha. You are making a mistake landing on
> the southern tip. If we capture Mdina in the north,
> we block off all communications and supplies for
> the castles.

> MUSTAPHA
>
> Do not forget the Sultan's expressed pleasure: I
> command the land forces. We are ashore, are we
> not?

> PIALI
>
> We were instructed to wait for Dragut.

> MUSTAPHA
>
> No doubt, Dragut will approve.
>
>   (pointing to map)
> We will travel inland and lay siege against the
> fortifications. Am I clear?

Piali burns, then turns sly.

> PIALI
>
> In which castle do you think your betrothed is
> held captive?

Mustapha almost takes the bait but doesn't.

> MUSTAPHA
>
> We are commanded by our Sultan to take siege of
> this island. I intend to do so.
>
>   (beat)
> We are the army of Allah. Who is there to stop us?

EXT. MALTA SOUTHERN SHORELINE, ROCKY RIDGE - NIGHT

Without warning, the shoreline explodes with knights on horseback. Ambush.

Copier leads his cavalry in assault on the unsuspecting Turks, scrambling for their weapons. Muskets CRACK. Turks go down. Few return volley.

INT. MUSTAPHA'S TENT - NIGHT

Piali and Mustapha are alerted by the sound of combat. They exit their tent.

EXT. MUSTAPHA'S TENT - NIGHT

A flaming arrow hits it and starts it afire. They try to assess the situation, but it's a mess.

> MUSTAPHA
> Withdraw! Withdraw!

The two generals charge to a waiting boat at the shoreline.

IN THE HEART OF THE BATTLE

Copier is Mars on horseback. He hammers and slices turbans. Pulls a pistol. Sends a screaming Janissary to Paradise.

He looks up. The Turkish Generals are fleeing. He glances at an officer next to him, RIVIÉRE, and screams in victory.

DISSOLVE TO:

AFTERMATH OF THE ASSAULT

The camp is obliterated. Smoldering ruins of carnage.

Knights finish off stragglers and trot around in victory on their snorting stallions. They gather around Copier.

> COPIER
> Well done, soldiers! We will kick these barbarian
> scoundrels right back to their stinking den of
> iniquity!

The cavalry CHEERS.

> RIVIÉRE
> Captain, look!

Copier looks where Riviére points. From the ships offshore, a thousand flickering lights. A huge armada of landing boats are returning to shore in vengeance.

> COPIER
> Back to the rocks and crags!

They depart to fight again.

As the last horseman vanishes, Riviére reappears to take one last look.

A JANISSARY looks up from playing dead on the ground. Riviére doesn't see him. The Janissary pops up and hammers Riviére on the back of the head with a mace. He goes down.

INT. LA VALETTE'S PRIVATE QUARTERS - NIGHT

La Valette reads a pamphlet by candlelight. He can't take his eyes from it. A knock at the door startles him.

> LA VALETTE
>> Enter.

It's Copier. He salutes.

> COPIER
>> Grand Master. We delayed their landing in Marsascirocco Bay.

> LA VALETTE
>> Their numbers?

> COPIER
>> Like the sand on the seashore.

La Valette drops, discouraged.

> LA VALETTE
>> Hold back within the fort and await further instruction.

La Valette returns to his desk duties. But Copier does not leave. La Valette looks up impatiently.

> COPIER
>> If I may, sir. I know Sandilands. He is the finest with incendiaries. And he is loyal to you.

> LA VALETTE
>> But not to the Pope.

> COPIER
>> We are going to need him, sir. Desperately.

>   LA VALETTE
>   Thank you, Copier.

Copier leaves, dejected.

La Valette glances down at the pamphlet he was looking at earlier. It is Sandilands' confiscated "Ninety-Five Theses" by Martin Luther.

INT. TURKISH SHORELINE CAMP - NIGHT

Riviére, the captured knight, is chained up in a Turkish tent, being "bastinadoed": feet and belly whipped mercilessly with a flogging cane. He cries out in anguish.

>   RIVIÉRE
>   Mercy! Mercy, please!!

Mustapha leans down to him with glee.

>   MUSTAPHA
>   I am waiting.

Then Mustapha smells something. He sniffs. Pulls back with a wrinkled nose. Aside to Piali.

>   MUSTAPHA
>   (in Turkish)
>   These Europeans stink like swine.

Piali smirks. Riviére gulps and against all his conscience, blurts out.

>   RIVIÉRE
>   Fort St. Elmo! It is the weakest castle!

Riviére bursts into tears. Mustapha pulls back and glares in triumph at Piali. But Riviére shatters the victory.

>   RIVIÉRE
>   Don Garcia from Sicily!

Mustapha spins around.

>   RIVIÉRE
>   On his way -- twenty-five thousand troops!

Piali gleams back at Mustapha.

PIALI
Tell me, Mustapha, what would Dragut approve
of now?

MUSTAPHA
(angry as all hell)
We do not have time to find out.

(to a messenger)
Call all troops. Double time to the Harbor!

INT. INQUISITOR'S PALACE, TORTURE CHAMBER - NIGHT

A red-headed SCOT screams in agony. He has met his threshold of pain on The Rack. His hands and feet stretched to their limit. Cartilage kneads apart.

Another crank by the ALGUAZIL, an Inquisitor Guard in white habit and black hood. The Redhead wails. Ignatius leans close to him and whispers.

IGNATIUS
Yes. Yes, my child. It is good to cry out. It is
cleansing for the soul.

The Redhead strains with all his might to regain his wits.

IGNATIUS
Dost thou have a confession?

The Redhead sputters. Ignatius leans closer.

REDHEAD
The Pope -- th-the Pope...

IGNATIUS
Yes, my son. You wish to declare allegiance to the
holy Pontiff?

REDHEAD
Th-the Pope -- is -- Antichrist.

Ignatius is scandalized. He walks away. Another crank. The Redhead bawls uncontrollably.

Ignatius approaches Sandilands, who is chained to The Chair. Spikes hold his neck and wrists in place. He draws blood trying to jump at the infernal devil before him.

> IGNATIUS
> Where is your Luther now, Sandilands? Bickering
> for control of your so-called "Reformation." You
> Protestants cannot even agree amongst
> yourselves.

> SANDILANDS
> I follow not Luther. I follow Christ.

> IGNATIUS
> You follow Satan!

Sandilands is unmoved. Ignatius signals another GUARD who mans The Hoist.

Another SCOT has his arms tied behind his back to a rope suspended from the ceiling by a pulley. The Guard pulls his rope and the Scot is hoisted into the air by his wrists behind him. He HOWLS in pain. The weight of his body dislocates his arms, tearing the joints apart.

Sandilands winces. He can't see his men this way.

And then the doors to the chamber CRASH open. Starkey and Romegas march in, horrified at the sight before them.

> ROMEGAS
> Sweet Mother of God.

> IGNATIUS
> How dare you interrupt me in the midst of holy
> labors!

> STARKEY
> This is madness.

La Valette storms in.

> LA VALETTE
> What are you doing to these men?

Sandilands looks helplessly at his rescuers. Ignatius regains his composure.

IGNATIUS

Grand Master. Be careful. Judge not what you
understand not.

LA VALETTE

I understand my soldiers are being tortured.

(to the knights with him)
Release them.

The knights jump. Sandilands looks with hope.

IGNATIUS

Halt! In the name of the Holy Office!

The knights stop. Look to La Valette for orders.

LA VALETTE

I want none of this on my island. I should have
you exiled.

Ignatius steps up to him.

IGNATIUS

This is not your island, La Valette. The Pope alone
has authority to remove me.

(he darkens with delight)
But giving aid to heretics? That is cause for
inquiry. And excommunication.

LA VALETTE

(unafraid)
It appears we have common privilege, Ignatius.
The Pope alone has authority to remove me.

STARKEY

Perhaps you two should have a talk with the
Pontiff to settle your differences.

This amuses Romegas. But not the trembling Ignatius. La Valette continues his
unmoving stare at Ignatius.

> IGNATIUS
> I warn you. If you free these men, you will incur
> the wrath of the Inquisition upon your head.

La Valette is unshaken by the serpent.

> LA VALETTE
> Ignatius. Move out of my way. Or I will cut you
> down.

Ignatius cowers like a rat. La Valette walks by him. His men lower the hoist, untie the poor Scots.

> LA VALETTE
> (to the guards)
> Keep this leech under watch.

The knights grab Ignatius. He squirms like a worm.

> LA VALETTE
> No correspondence is to leave the island under his
> title or authority.

> IGNATIUS
> I protest! I protest!

They carry him away. La Valette releases Sandilands.

> SANDILANDS
> Thank you, Grand Master, for freeing us.

> LA VALETTE
> I did not say I was freeing you.

INT. CASTLE DUNGEON, MALTA - DARK

A cast iron door opens, and Sandilands is thrown into a dungeon cell. La Valette is at the door.

The door slams shut, leaving Sandilands alone in darkness.

P.O.V. MOUNT SCIBERRAS THROUGH A SPYGLASS - DAY

Through a spyglass across the Harbor, La Valette watches a long train of Turkish soldiers trudge over the rocky terrain of Mount Sciberras and set up camp. Slaves roll cannons into battery position overlooking Fort St. Elmo. Impending doom. Next to La Valette, Starkey, Copier and Romegas.

> ROMEGAS
> How many stationed at St. Elmo, sir?

> LA VALETTE
> Eight hundred. All we can spare.

> COPIER
> How many Turks reckon you?

La Valette looks to Starkey.

> STARKEY
> Ten thousand.

EXT. SOUTHERN SHORELINE TURKISH CAMP, MALTA - NIGHT

Several Turkish galleys pull silently up to land. In the lead of the arriving soldiers is Dragut, The Sword of Allah.

INT. MUSTAPHA'S TENT, BACK LINES

Mustapha and Piali consult a map. A Recon Soldier enters the tent. The Generals look up.

EXT. MUSTAPHA'S TENT

Mustapha and Piali exit the tent. Dragut marches up to them, with his corps of soldiers. They salute.

> MUSTAPHA
> Mighty Dragut!

> DRAGUT
> What in the name of Allah are you doing?

Mustapha looks at Piali.

> MUSTAPHA
> Why, preparing for your arrival.

                    DRAGUT
        You fools. Why did you not seize the city of
        Mdina in the north first?!

                    PIALI
        My sentiments exactly, Dragut.

Mustapha gives Piali a look of betrayal.

                    MUSTAPHA
        Our intelligence told us otherwise.

                    DRAGUT
        Stupidity told you otherwise! This castle is
        isolated from all strategic locations. Its mound is
        too rocky for mines, and water assault is
        unfeasible!

Mustapha is disgraced.

                    PIALI
        Mustapha's captive was not entirely honest with
        him.

Another betrayal by Piali registers on Mustapha's face. Dragut considers his
options for a moment. Then...

                    DRAGUT
        We have lost far too much time. Begin
        bombardment immediately. Sustain it through the
        night. And bring this captive to me.

A guard whisks off. Dragut looks with disgust at Mustapha's ostentatious silk
tent and ornamental display.

                    DRAGUT
        Pompous pigs. I will be housing with the artillery
        squad.

He leaves. Piali smirks at the humiliated Mustapha.

EXT. TURKISH CANNON BATTERY

Mustapha tramps down the line commanding firing. Soldiers jump up and begin to powder and load their cannons.

EXT. MUSTAPHA'S TENT

A guard brings the captive knight Riviére and throws him at Dragut's feet. The pathetic shell of a once great warrior. Dragut looks curiously at Riviére. Draws his scimitar and beheads him with one sweep.

AND THE CANNONS BEGIN TO ROAR.

EXT. ST. ELMO'S - NIGHT

SUPER: MAY 28

Knights on the ravelin wall awaken to the sound of CANNON. The ravelin and castle are pounded by 50 and 100 pound balls of iron and marble.

Round after round, an unending stream of bombardment picks away at the rock barrier.

INT. ST. ELMO'S FORTRESS - NIGHT

Soldiers everywhere run for cover as cannonballs make it inside the castle. Structures are demolished upon impact.

EXT. FORT BIRGU - NIGHT

Across the water, La Valette, Starkey, Romegas, Copier and a host of soldiers stand silently observing the pyrotechnic display. These are their brothers being hammered.

DISSOLVE TO:

EXT. ST. ELMO'S RAVELIN WALL - DAY

The artillery continues strafing the walls. It's been going on for days. The ravelin and castle walls are swiss cheese. Soldiers hide anywhere they can, their morale blown to pieces.

Cannons on the castle wall fire back but are dwarfed by the Turkish fusillade. One of them is demolished by a hit.

EXT. FORT BIRGU - DAY

La Valette silently eats alone. The sound of distant cannons deadens his appetite. A KNOCK at the door. Starkey, Copier and Romegas enter.

> ROMEGAS
> Grand Master, that is the sound of our defenses
> being bludgeoned.

> COPIER
> When those pagans assail the fort, there will not
> be anything left to stop them. Except a good
> incendiary strategy.

La Valette looks at Starkey.

> STARKEY
> I am afraid they are right, sir. We need to even up
> the odds.

La Valette stares at them angrily. He knows they're right.

INT. CASTLE DUNGEON, MALTA - DARK

Sandilands can hear the percussion of the artillery even down here. He prays for his brethren. A guard approaches.

> GUARDS
> Up, Sandilands!

Sandilands moves. The door opens and La Valette is there with a plate of food and water. He hands it to Sandilands, who devours it voraciously.

> LA VALETTE
> St. Elmo is under siege.

Sandilands stops.

> SANDILANDS
> I am sure the Grand Master is thoroughly
> prepared for such a strategy.

La Valette doesn't answer. He's troubled by something else.

LA VALETTE
I have always considered indulgences to be
problematical myself.

Sandilands is startled. Then grabs his chance.

SANDILANDS
"When a coin in the coffer rings, another soul from
purgatory springs." -- Lies.

LA VALETTE
But why the hostility of this - Luther, and his
"Reformation?"

SANDILANDS
Who is persecuting whom, m'lord?

LA VALETTE
But defiance against the Holy Father.

SANDILANDS
Jesus said we have but one Father who is in
heaven.

La Valette is irritated.

LA VALETTE
What of this accusation of -- devil worship?

SANDILANDS
I worship One God the Father and his only
begotten Son, Jesus Christ, the Redeemer. Is that
devil worship?

LA VALETTE
The Holy Roman Empire has lasted for over a
thousand years.

SANDILANDS
It is a new world, m'lord. -- And God is in control.

LA VALETTE
Why do you wish to fight for me if my religion is
so intolerable to you?

> SANDILANDS
> With respect, sir. The winds of reform blow strong
> through Europe. I fight to preserve that purity.

> LA VALETTE
> The enemy of my enemy is my ally.

> SANDILANDS
> Grand Master. You are not my enemy. The
> servants of Mohammed are my enemies.

La Valette looks at Sandilands. Adversaries united.

EXT. ST. ELMO SHORELINE - NIGHT

The artillery continues. A galley carrying 50 knights secretly reaches the shores of St. Elmo. Romegas in the lead. Next to him, Sandilands and his crew. Freed.

In Sandilands' hands, the banned pamphlet by Luther returned to him. In his eyes, a holy fire.

The galley reaches the shore. Sandilands and the others slip into the water. Their destination: St. Elmo, towering in the background.

Romegas heads back with his ships.

INT. ST. ELMO'S FORTRESS - EARLY MORNING

Under the ongoing FLAK, Sandilands and his men wheel cauldrons over the small bridge to the ravelin walls.

He directs men carrying the copper trumps to spread them out along the ridge. And others with hand grenades and hoops.

DISSOLVE TO:

EXT. ST. ELMO'S FORTRESS - LATER

The knights and soldiers, spirits defeated, hide under the incessant barrage. The ground strewn with cannonballs.

And then it all stops. An eerie silence. Ears are ringing.

Sandilands looks over the wall. On distant Sciberras, an IMAM, holy man, YELLS and the BUZZ of crowds respond.

> SANDILANDS
> They are praying.

EXT. TURKISH CAMP - DAY

All around the Turkish camp, soldiers kneel on carpets facing eastward to Mecca and recite prayers led by the Imams.

EXT. ST. ELMO'S RAVELIN WALL - DAY

Soldiers roll dice and chew on jerky. The distant prayer chanting stops.

Again, eerie silence.

Sandilands steps up to the ravelin wall and the soldiers watch for movement.

Nothing.

And then, the piercing "ULULING" of kamikaze soldiers called IAYALARS fills the air.

Sandilands yells to his men.

> SANDILANDS
> Iayalars! Get ready for a paddling, lads!

Sandilands' assistant helps him move a pot to the wall.

They ready the trump tubes and fill them with the chemical mixture from earlier. Torches at the ready.

> ASSISTANT
> What are they?

> SANDILANDS
> Religious fanatics. They smoke hashish to become
> fearless.
>
> > (he peers darkly at him)
> They are expendable.

The Assistant gulps. And over the hilltop run a thousand SCREAMING banshees robed in white, scimitars gleaming, ready to die for glory.

The knights fire musket and cannon into the attacking forces. It's only a nuisance to the mass of marauders.

They reach the ravelin wall. Throw up ladders and make their ascent.

They keep coming, wave after unending wave.

> SANDILANDS
> Give 'em their first taste of hell, lads!

Large hoops carried to the edge by tongs. The hoop is lit on fire and dropped on the climbing Turks.

Their turbans and flowing robes are kindling. The hoops trap two or three together. Searing flesh. Plummeting bodies.

Torches light grenades. Grenades are thrown and burst on impact, putting aflame their screaming victims. Human torches.

But the drugged invaders are unyielding. So, Sandilands pours on his big guns: "Wildfire." The cauldrons are lit and poured onto the mass of men, burning up scores of them in a blazing river of fire. Sandilands yells out above the fray.

> SANDILANDS
> Welcome to the Lake of Fire, ye devils!

The trumps belch out fireballs that fly thirty feet, catching their victims on the run in a burst of flames.

A knight lights a grenade. It explodes in his hands and covers his armor in flames. He screams. Backs up and jumps into a waiting tub of water, dousing the fire from his body.

Finally, the BLOW OF A TRUMPET. The Turks are slaughtered. They withdraw.

And the knights CHEER.

Thousands of charred smoldering corpses litter the base of the ravelin. Massacre.

Across the channel at Fort Birgu, huge flags unfurl and war drums BEAT.

They CHEER again.

EXT. FORT BIRGU - DAY

La Valette and his soldiers, under the heavy beat of their war drums, cheer on their brothers.

But the CANNONADE begins again, shattering the knights' short-lived victory.

INT. FORT BIRGU FOOD PANTRY - DAY

Multitudes of begging villagers crowd the window.

Selima, still veiled, hands out what food she can with several other chaplain knights. Her heart goes out to these poor wretches. They didn't ask for all this.

> SELIMA
> Please! Please! We will have more tomorrow!

She bumps up against a knight. He pulls back in disgust. She's a leper to the holy. But she continues anyway.

INT. SACRED INFIRMARY HALLWAY, FORT BIRGU - NIGHT

Selima plods to her room, exhausted. The sound of CANNONS still in the background. Starkey slips out of the shadows and hushes her.

> SELIMA
> I feared the worst for you.

> STARKEY
> So, you do care for me?

She pulls back, cold.

> SELIMA
> I respect you.

He reaches up to her veil.

This time, she lets him uncover her face.

He moves to kiss her. She balks.

He starts again, and she willingly tastes him.

He looks at her, dizzy.

> STARKEY
> Do you still respect me?

> SELIMA
> You are an unusual man. You suffer intolerance
> for your vows to God, yet you cast those same
> vows aside for the affections of an "infidel slave."

> STARKEY
> Selima, I have not been entirely honest with you
> about my history.

Before he can explain, a voice shatters their focus.

> HOSPITALLER (O.S.)
> Selima!

The HEAD HOSPITALLER bounds around the corner. He sees Selima in Starkey's arms. Caught in the act.

Starkey slips away into the darkness, leaving Selima there.

> HOSPITALLER
> I need your help in the ward, now!

INT. SACRED INFIRMARY WARD, FORT BIRGU - DAY

They enter the sick ward. Several wounded knights are brought in on stretchers. The Hospitaller waves her over.

> HOSPITALLER
> The wounded from St. Elmo. Wash your hands,
> quickly! Always wash your hands.

She does so in the basin before her. He holds out a compress.

> HOSPITALLER
> Take this compress and hold it tightly to the
> wound.

She sees a huge gouge ripping the knight's leg.

She reaches for it. The knight holds up his dagger, halting her.

> KNIGHT
> I will not be touched by this - heathen wench.

> HOSPITALLER
> (impatiently)
> Then you will die.

The knight balks.

> HOSPITALLER
> And you will enter Purgatory to burn off all your
> sins. Including those of pride and intolerance.

The knight hesitates. Reluctantly lowers his dagger.

Selima catches the Hospitaller's eyes. He moves on.

She presses. The knight HOWLS in pain. She winces in empathy.

The Head Hospitaller notices Starkey at the entrance watching her from the distance.

INT. ST. ELMO'S FORTRESS - DAY

Sandilands checks his supply of incendiary weapons in a shelter stocked with piles of them. One of his men enters.

> KNIGHT
> Sir! They are shooting fireballs.

Sandilands steps out of the storeroom. He sees fireballs careening through the sky.

And then a huge one comes right at them! They hit the dirt as the ball hits the storeroom, BLOWING IT TO SMITHEREENS.

Sandilands crawls away, barely escaping with his life. He looks at the blazing inferno.

> SANDILANDS
> We're fooked.

And then another RUMBLE SOUND. But this one is not from mortars. It's a thundercloud overhead.

EXT. ST. ELMO'S RAVELIN - NIGHT

Rain floods the landscape. The cannons have stopped. Knights wait, drenched by the downpour. Some keep cover.

A SENTRY on watch stands by an opening lookout onto the empty terrain. He's asleep on his feet, quietly snoring away. Another Guard down the way looks over at him and whispers.

> GUARD
> How looks it down there?

The snoring Sentry jostles awake and waves to the Guard.

EXT. ST. ELMO OUTER TERRAIN

In the darkness, outside the ravelin wall, a lone TURKISH BOWMAN, hidden behind a rock, sees the Sentry up on the wall.

He aims his crossbow and releases.

EXT. ST. ELMO'S RAVELIN WALL

The Sentry is struck in the heart by the silent missile. He leans against the wall without falling. Dead.

Sandilands crosses the ravelin bridge from the castle wall in the rain and approaches the Guard.

>   SANDILANDS
>   Any signs?

The Guard glances over at the dead Sentry who seems alive leaning on the wall.

The Guard shakes his head. Sandilands returns to the castle.

EXT. ST. ELMO OUTER TERRAIN

Outside the ravelin wall, a contingent of Turks silently climb the walls with ladders.

EXT. ST. ELMO'S RAVELIN WALL

The Guard checks on the Sentry. He falls over, an arrow in his heart.

The Guard looks over the wall. Sees the ascending Turks. Raises his rifle. But it won't trigger in the pouring rain.

He's hit by an arrow. Staggers.

>   SOLDIERS
>   BREACH!! BREEEEEEACH!!!!

He stumbles backward and falls to his death in the ditch.

The knights rise up as the Turks jump over the wall and the battle begins.

Swords, shields, maces, scimitars.

A soldier grabs a grenade and opens a cauldron.

But his torch is soaking wet and burnt out. No use. He drops it and pulls his sword, screaming.

EXT. ST. ELMO'S FORTRESS - DAY

Sandilands arrives at the bridge to see the ravelin wall teeming with Turks.

He shouts and crosses, others close behind.

But it's too late. The Turks are on top. They're pushing over cauldrons and throwing the last of the hoops and trumps into the ditch below.

Sandilands and his men are pushed back on the bridge. The way is narrow, the fighting intense. Sword for sword, they're losing.

A knight next to Sandilands is shot dead by an arrow. Sandilands screams behind his fighting unit.

> SANDILANDS
> Drop the bridge!

The Turks have almost reached the castle side. Sandilands is the last on the bridge. It's almost over.

> SANDILANDS
> Drop the bridge! Now!

Soldiers by the wall pull ropes.

Underneath the bridge, the ropes are connected to key struts. They snap.

Sandilands leaps to safety.

The bridge falls to the ditch below, carrying a squad of Turks to their deaths.

The knights HOOT and CHEER. But their deliverance is short. The Turks have captured the ravelin. Their TAUNTING JEERS drown the knights' confidence.

INT. SACRED INFIRMARY WARD - DAY

Selima and other orderlies attend to the numerous wounded in the ward. They can barely keep up with the needs.

She sees a groaning knight laid on a surgery table, his bowels pressing out of a stomach wound. He won't make it.

INT. SACRED INFIRMARY WARD - LATER, DUSK

The ward is calm. Patients sleep. Selima stands and looks out the window at the far-off glow and tremor of battle at St. Elmo. She is in tears for the madness.

EXT. FORT BIRGU SHORELINE - DUSK

Through his spyglass, Starkey sees the ravelin built up with dirt and cannons wheeled onto it by slaves. Fifty yards to the castle walls. It's going to be an absolute slaughter.

He lowers the glass. Before him, a battle-worn messenger from St. Elmo on the beach. La Valette, Romegas and a battalion of anxious soldiers stand by.

> MESSENGER
> Sire. It has been over three weeks. Our water is
> low. No ammunition. Fifty knights and not a one
> of them unscathed. The walls will soon be ground
> to powder.

> LA VALETTE
> The safety of the island lies in holding out as many
> days as possible.

The Messenger is chagrined. La Valette is not listening.

> STARKEY
> Grand Master. To stay will mean sure death for
> all. Withdraw and they can fight another day.

> LA VALETTE
> Every day incurs greater chance of Don Garcia's
> arrival with reinforcements.

Starkey can't contain himself.

> STARKEY
> For God's sake, sir! Their deaths are useless to our
> cause! You do not actually have faith in that
> Sicilian whoremonger?!

> LA VALETTE
> Sir Oliver. You are a fine advisor. But your
> pragmatism will be your undoing.

Starkey backs down in shame before his fellow officers. The Messenger holds out a piece of paper to La Valette.

> MESSENGER
> All the knights but three have signed this paper
> urging the Grand Master to reconsider his
> command.

This pierces La Valette right to the soul. Near mutiny.

Even Starkey and Romegas are shocked.

La Valette crumples the paper in defiance.

> LA VALETTE
> You will tell the knights they are to hold the castle
> to the last man. To the last drop of blood.

> MESSENGER
> Yes, sire.

He turns to leave.

> LA VALETTE
> Bailiff!

> MESSENGER
> Yes, sir.

> LA VALETTE
> Tell them... I will do so as well.

The Messenger straightens with trust and respect for his Grand Master. He jumps into his skiff back to St. Elmo.

La Valette painfully feels the weight of his own commands.

> STARKEY
> So much for chivalry.

La Valette looks at him with contempt.

> ROMEGAS
> Sir. Who were the three unsigned patriots,
> unwilling to leave?

La Valette regains his pride.

> LA VALETTE
> Sandilands and his Protestants.

Romegas is impressed to the soul.

La Valette turns to his crowd of waiting knights.

> LA VALETTE
> I want fifty volunteers willing to take the place of
> the knights at St. Elmo.

Starkey and Romegas look at each other in astonishment.

> LA VALETTE
> You will relieve your brothers, who have
> protected you thus far. And will most assuredly
> die defending the fort.

The knights are taken aback.

But slowly, hands are raised.

From the back, steps a MALTESE NOBLE. A band of his fellow aristocrats follow him. These were the ones who had complained earlier. Now, repentant.

> MALTESE NOBLE
> It would be an honor to die for our country. And
> for freedom from the Turks.

La Valette looks victoriously at Starkey.

> LA VALETTE
> So much for your "new world."

EXT. MOUNT SCIBERRAS GENERAL'S CAMP - DUSK

Dragut sees La Valette and the crowd of knights on the beach through his spyglass. Behind him, Mustapha and Piali.

> DRAGUT
> How goes the artillery on the ravelin wall?

> MUSTAPHA
> Completed and awaiting command.

> DRAGUT
> Prepare for final assault.

Mustapha and Piali march away.

Under his breath, Piali taunts Mustapha.

> PIALI
> I must compliment you, Mustapha. You are quite
> the commander. With the help of course, of
> Dragut's humble "advice."

Mustapha boils. There's nothing he can do about it.

EXT. ST. ELMO'S RAVELIN WALL - NIGHT -

> SUPER: JUNE 23

Point blank Turkish cannons pulverize the castle walls fifty yards away. Soon there will be no walls.

EXT. ST. ELMO'S FORTRESS - NIGHT

On the cliffside of the castle, FIFTY KNIGHTS secret their way up the treacherous crags to the castle base.

INT. ST. ELMO'S HOSPITAL WARD - NIGHT

The place is filled with dead and wounded. GROANS of pain. Calls for help. Fellow knights tend as best they can through the shaking of cannon salvo.

Sandilands lays with a head wound on a cot, his leg broken.

The few who can stand are gathered around as fifty reserve knights, led by Romegas, step up to the Messenger and his COMMANDING OFFICER, a bloody mess himself.

> COMMANDING OFFICER
> Reinforcements?

> ROMEGAS
> Replacements.

The Officer is stunned.

From behind Romegas, a knight steps forth in royal armor. La Valette himself!

> COMMANDING OFFICER
> Grand Master! Your life is in danger here!

La Valette looks upon each and every knight there. And then, with slow cool sarcasm...

> LA VALETTE
> Captain, I have with me older, more trustworthy
> knights of the Order. They have no concern for the
> preservation of their lives and have only complete
> loyalty to their Grand Master. We have all, to the
> man, decided to take your place and protect you
> so that you may live.

Sandilands smiles at the bravado. Others are not so amused.

> LA VALETTE
> Because you are so mightily concerned for the
> preservation of your own lives, it behooves me to
> allow you safe passage to the comfort and protection
> of your brethren across the harbor. Should any wish
> not to be replaced, step forward and an equal
> number of us will return to Birgu. Otherwise, off
> with you. We soldiers have a job to do.

The St. Elmo knights glower in shame.

The Commanding Officer steps forward, kneels at La Valette's feet.

> COMMANDING OFFICER
> Forgive me, m'lord.

One by one, every one of the St. Elmo knights steps forward with their Commanding Officer.

Sandilands CHEERS and the others follow suit.

La Valette regains his pride in his knights' honor.

EXT. ST. ELMO'S FORTRESS - NIGHT

Cannonballs whizz by and destroy the remaining vestiges of the castle interior. There's hardly anything left.

And then it all stops. Calm before the storm.

Through the dust and debris, the St. Elmo knights and their foot-soldiers, 100 strong, take their places in the yard for battle.

Sandilands has himself carried out on a chair to fight to the end.

They wait.

The unnerving Turkish WAILS begin and through the crumbled remains of castle wall, they come. Like an army of fire ants wild with rage. Unstoppable.

Muskets CRACK. Men go down. The knights are incredible for their part, taking out three for every man.

Sandilands staves off several of them from his chair. But he is overtaken and run through with a sword.

Dying on the ground, he looks up into heaven.

> SANDILANDS
> Save your people, Lord.

EXT. ST. ELMO'S SHORELINE - NIGHT

La Valette and his fifty men row back to Birgu in silent respect for their fallen comrades.

INT. ST. ELMO'S FORTRESS - DAY

A Turk throws the flag with Cross of St. John into the dust and hoists the Star and Crescent up the flagpole.

Dragut tramps through the debris of bodies and rubble, followed by Piali. He surveys the damage. There's not much left of the place.

He looks back upon the lay of battle. Thousands dead. Mostly his own.

> DRAGUT
> What are the casualties?

> MUSTAPHA
> Fifteen hundred or so knights. None have been
> spared.

> DRAGUT
> And of our own?

> PIALI
> By my count, eight thousand.

> DRAGUT
>
> Eight thousand pities. What will the father's price
> be, with so costly a son?
>
> > (a painful beat)
>
> Gather all these Christian savages together.

INT. ST. ELMO'S FORTRESS INFIRMARY - DAY

Mustapha walks with focused purpose through the debris and bodies, followed by a MONSTER of a soldier. He is looking for something. Someone.

He pinpoints a wounded knight barely alive. He gestures to Monster, who reaches in the rubble and pulls the bloody knight up. His arm is blown to shreds.

Monster swings him around like a rag doll to face the uncaring eyes of Mustapha.

> MUSTAPHA
>
> Where is the Sultan's harem?

The knight doesn't speak. Monster squeezes him. His ribs CRUNCH. He spits up blood.

> MUSTAPHA
>
> > (unflinching)
>
> Where is the Sultan's harem?

> KNIGHT
>
> S-s-Sen-glea.

A subtle satisfaction dawns on Mustapha's face. He walks away.

Monster grins and squeezes the Knight. His bones CRACK under the crushing embrace and he breathes his last.

EXT. FORT BIRGU - DAY

Starkey oversees the carving of spikes out of small tree trunks. A messenger interrupts him.

> MESSENGER
>
> Sir Oliver. The Grand Master bids you come.

EXT. FORT BIRGU SHORELINE - DAY

Starkey is at the shoreline, sick to his stomach, with La Valette, Romegas, and a host of knights.

The harbor is clogged with the bodies of the St. Elmo knights nailed to drifting crucifixes of wood. They're headless and have their hearts ripped out of their chests.

>   ROMEGAS
>   That spawn of hell.

La Valette is trance-like.

Starkey cannot say a word.

>   LA VALETTE
>   Starkey. Show me to the Turkish prisoners.

They leave the gruesome scene of carnage.

INT. CASTLE DUNGEON - DARK

A large cell. Torches and eerie shadows. Ottoman prisoners in robes and turbans. Chattering Turkish.

The cell door opens. La Valette and Starkey appear at the door glaring in.

EXT. FORT BIRGU - DAY

Cannons are lit toward St. Elmo and fire across the harbor.

EXT. ST. ELMO'S FORTRESS - DAY

Turkish soldiers run to the wall to see. But these are no cannonballs. They hit the ground like sacks of dirt.

Dragut steps out of his command post. A soldier steps up to him.

In each hand, he holds a smoldering decapitated turbaned head! La Valette's reply to Dragut.

Dragut grabs one of the heads. Holds it up and vows to it.

> DRAGUT
> I promise you that not one single knight shall
> leave this island alive. Save this La Valette, who
> shall bow before the Sultan and lick his feet.

He tosses the head in the dirt and walks away.

Mustapha watches him in trepidation.

INT. SACRED INFIRMARY WARD, FORT BIRGU - DAY

Selima finishes changing bedsheets. She sees the belongings of the previous patient. Coins, crucifix, a dried flower, probably from a lover.

She holds it, dreaming. And then a pamphlet. "Ninety Five Theses" by Martin Luther. She looks around. Slips the flower and pamphlet into her gown.

And Starkey is there. He smiles.

EXT. SACRED INFIRMARY GARDEN - NIGHT

Starkey and Selima walk in the Infirmary garden under moonlight. Starkey looks forlorn.

> SELIMA
> What ails you?

> STARKEY
> The Grand Master. With each defeat, his resolve
> grows stronger.

> SELIMA
> Such things are not for the ears of a captive.

> STARKEY
> I do not care anymore. It is becoming increasingly
> foolish to me.

> SELIMA
> Foolish to die for one's faith?

> STARKEY
> More wise to live for it.

SELIMA
You are a man of divided loyalties.

Starkey searches for the strength to tell her.

STARKEY
Selima, when I told you that I was persecuted for
my faith, I was not telling you the whole truth.
(beat)
I had fallen in love with a woman.

Selima's interest is piqued.

STARKEY
I defied my king for honor but betrayed my Order
for love. So, I am a man of divided loyalties. And
it has torn my heart asunder.

SELIMA
Where is she now?

STARKEY
She died. While I was rotting in jail.

Selima draws near to him. He pulls her closer.

STARKEY
The taste of blood and war has made me weary.
(beat)
But when I am with you, I taste healing for the
first time in my life.

SELIMA
The beginning of healing is finding one's wounds.

Starkey pulls away shamefully.

STARKEY
I have slain many a Muslim, your brother.

SELIMA
Many a Muslim have slain your brother.

He looks at her. But she withdraws.

>   STARKEY
>   (without conviction)
>   A soldier's duty is to fight.

>   SELIMA
>   A Christian's duty is to love.

It stops him. She hands him the dry flower she found earlier. He accepts it.

Grabs her in a violent explosion of desire. They smother each other in a barrage of kisses.

INT. SELIMA'S ROOM, SACRED INFIRMARY - NIGHT

Starkey, naked and vulnerable, lowers himself gently onto Selima's quivering form. His fury tamed by love. And for a moment in time, all the world is of no consequence.

EXT. TURKISH ENCAMPMENT OUTSIDE BIRGU AND SENGLEA - DAY

The Turks roll their cannons in place overlooking forts Senglea and Birgu, two peninsula castles side by side. Preparations for the next phase of attack.

EXT. MALTA COASTLINE - NIGHT

A barricade of Turkish galleys spreads out off the coast, lights glowing.

On the beach, a small, lean sailing boat lands in the darkness. Salvago hops out in stealth.

INT. GRAND MASTER'S PRIVATE ROOM, MALTA - DAY

Starkey sits with La Valette as Salvago wolfs down a meal.

>   SALVAGO
>   The Viceroy has decided to send twenty-thousand
>   reinforcements.

>   STARKEY
>   Down from twenty-five.

Salvago darkens.

>   SALVAGO
>   But he asks in return that you send him your
>   galleys.

Starkey looks at La Valette in disbelief.

>LA VALETTE
>
> He knows I cannot afford the men it takes to sail those vessels.

>STARKEY
>
> Not to mention the impossibility of sailing a fleet out through the blockade.

>LA VALETTE
>
> Return to Don Garcia and tell him I cannot spare him the men he requests.

Salvago is finished. He stands.

>SALVAGO
>
> Yes, sir.

And he's off. Starkey looks over at La Valette.

>STARKEY
>
> Grand Master. May I speak with you?

La Valette looks at him.

INT. GRAND MASTER'S PRIVATE CHAMBERS - NIGHT

Starkey and La Valette stand off in a contest of wills.

>STARKEY
>
> Sir, I implore you. Now is the time to negotiate.

>LA VALETTE
>
> With the devil himself?

>STARKEY
>
> Our backs are up against the castle walls. We have nowhere to go and no one to help us.

>LA VALETTE
>
> Would you prefer a return to your Protestant England? Or does your "tolerance" not extend that far?

>   STARKEY
> That is not the point. We will be slaughtered.

>   LA VALETTE
> Self-preservation is not the point, Sir Oliver. You
> forget. These are pagans arrayed against the army
> of the Lord. Our very God is blasphemed.

>   STARKEY
> And so, they consider us pagans. And we are
> blasphemers to their god. We are no different than
> them. We are but on opposite sides.

>   LA VALETTE
> One of us must be right.

>   STARKEY
> Or all of us are wrong.

La Valette will not respond.

EXT. TURKISH SIEGE ENCAMPMENT - DAY

The Turks are lined up behind their basilisks, staring down upon the walls of Fort Senglea.

Between the besiegers and castle is a small tent guarded by both knights and Turks. A white flag flies over it.

EXT. NEGOTIATIONS TENT - DAY

La Valette and Starkey approach the tent with armed guard.

>   STARKEY
> Please remember, sir. These are negotiations.
> Consider the pragmatics of our situation.

>   LA VALETTE
> Secretary Starkey. Your "pragmatics" are
> beginning to agitate me.

>   STARKEY
> The Good Book says, "Pride cometh before a fall,"
> sir.

>LA VALETTE
>It also says, "The fool hath said in his heart, There
>is no God."

Starkey backs down. They continue on into the tent.

INT. NEGOTIATIONS TENT - DAY

Inside, Starkey and La Valette stand before a vainglorious array of servants and decor.

>LA VALETTE
>These Turks reek of curry and incense.

And then Dragut enters, flanked by Piali and Mustapha, with Monster not far behind. At last they meet.

Dragut eyes La Valette with a mixture of respect and hatred.

Starkey mutters to La Valette.

>STARKEY
>Dragut, the sword of Islam.

>LA VALETTE
>The scourge of God.

Dragut cackles in Turkish to an INTERPRETER.

>INTERPRETER
>Mighty Dragut, the honorable, says you have
>proven a difficult adversary. He applauds you.
>   (Dragut speaks)
>Nevertheless, surrender now and the Sultan offers
>you honors of war with safe passage.

>STARKEY
>How kindhearted of him.

>LA VALETTE
>Tell your sovereign, I intend to stand firm, and let
>all of Islam march down upon us. We will not
>surrender.

Starkey looks incredulously at the stubborn La Valette.

STARKEY
Grand Master...

LA VALETTE
Shut up, secretary.

INTERPRETER
(without speaking to Dragut)
You are a fool. You will all die.

LA VALETTE
Tell him.

The Interpreter does. Dragut responds.

INTERPRETER
Then so be it. This was his personal preference
anyway.

La Valette burns with indignation.

Dragut speaks again to the Interpreter.

DRAGUT
(in Turkish with subtitles)
I will destroy them to the last man.

LA VALETTE
(in Turkish)
We will stand to the last man.

His Turkish surprises the Interpreter. But not Dragut.

LA VALETTE
(Turkish)
I was a slave on your infernal galleys.

DRAGUT
(in English)
And I, yours. And may I remind the Grand Master
and his knights of St. John of their defeat at
Rhodes but 40 years ago.

This punctures a deep wound in La Valette. Starkey can see it.

Dragut smirks.

> LA VALETTE
> (Turkish)
> I will never bow the knee to your Sultan.

A lingering pause.

> DRAGUT
> (English)
> Oh, but you will.

EXT. NEGOTIATIONS TENT - DAY

La Valette storms back to the castle. Starkey and his men barely keep pace with him.

INT. LA VALETTE'S WAR ROOM

Starkey stands at attention before La Valette, who sits at his desk reading a document.

He looks up from reading. Starkey looks straight ahead, unflinching. He reads on.

> LA VALETTE
> "...cannot in good conscience continue to support
> the Grand Master..."
>
> (looks up again at Starkey)
> Conscience? Sir Oliver, when did you receive back
> your conscience from the dead? I thought your
> "New World" was about "pragmatics," not moral
> scruples.

Starkey can no longer hold it in. He explodes.

> STARKEY
> Sir. The Crusades are long over. We Hospitallers
> are the last of a dying breed. The Teutons, the
> Templars are all disbanded. We alone are left.

> LA VALETTE
> Thanks to the Inquisition.

STARKEY

It is all a pretense for power. Yet you cling to this archaic notion of "chivalry and honor."

LA VALETTE

You would prefer I cower like a live rat.

STARKEY

I would prefer you negotiate for the lives of your men!

LA VALETTE

The lives of the few for the many.

STARKEY

Is that really what you want, Sir? To get us all killed?

La Valette is lost in thought. He is taken away in a memory.

LA VALETTE

I was there in Rhodes. A mere youth of twenty seven years. We were surrounded by the Sultan's forces. We held the island for five months. Outnumbered ten to one.

(beat)

The Grand Master surrendered. The armies of the Living God humiliated by blasphemers. Dragut was there. In his eyes I saw the fires of hell. And in my heart, I knew that one day I would face him again. Henceforth, I swore by Christ that if I became Grand Master of the Order, we would never again surrender. Never.

La Valette's eyes are red with anger.

Starkey remains resolved.

STARKEY

This thirst for martyrdom. Is it courage? -- Or pride?

La Valette will not look at him.

> LA VALETTE
> This advice of yours. Is it strategy -- or your
> newly-found love of the enemy?

Starkey drops in disgrace.

> LA VALETTE
> The Head Hospitaller told me.

> STARKEY
> Sir. She is not the enemy.

> LA VALETTE
> She is an idolater.

> STARKEY
> I would never compromise my Order -- or the
> lives of its men.

La Valette eyes him suspiciously.

> LA VALETTE
> What about your faith?

> STARKEY
> I would also not allow intolerance to blind my
> judgement.

La Valette is stung by the jab. But he hardens with resolve.

> LA VALETTE
> Secretary. Intolerance is a universal inevitability. It
> is merely a question of what one is intolerant of.

> STARKEY
> With due respect, sir. I cannot approve of this
> suicidal indiscretion.

> LA VALETTE
> Then we will do it without you.

Starkey stiffens to attention.

> STARKEY
> Please accept my request for reassignment to
> administrative services.

La Valette takes a heavy sigh.

> LA VALETTE
> I have a much better idea.

INT. SPARSE JAIL CELL, BIRGU - DAY

Starkey kneels naked on the stone floor. A MONK raises a flogging stick with leather straps. CRACK! It slaps against Starkey's back, bleeding with the stripes of forty lashes.

INT. FOOD PANTRY, FORT SENGLEA - DAY

Starkey, still bruised from his flogging, and dressed in rags, is tossed about in the pantry with the other chaplains. He gives food to the pressing numbers of poor outside.

> THE POOR
> Please, sir! Please, sir! Have mercy! God bless the
> Knights of St. John!

Starkey hands out the food. He sees their desperation. Their utter gratefulness.

A CRAGGY one meets his gaze.

> CRAG
> Slaughter those heathen swine. Eh, sir?

But Starkey can only stare at the man.

INT. DRAGUT'S TENT - NIGHT

Torchlight. Dragut, Mustapha and Piali plan their next siege. On the map, a diagram of the two side-by-side peninsulas and their forts. Dragut traces his strategy over the map.

> DRAGUT
> We will take Senglea first. Mustapha prepare your
> Janissaries for the ravelin.

                    PIALI
                (jealous)
            What about me?

                    DRAGUT
            Fear not, Piali. You will have your chance for sea
            battle.

Piali brightens.

                    DRAGUT
            The great chain and Birgu's firepower are too
            strong for harbor approach. You will portage ships
            over land into the harbor basin, here.

He points to the inner bay away from the forts.

Piali's countenance drops.

                    PIALI
            Portage?

                    DRAGUT
            Three point assault -- by land, by sea. And by the
            guns of St. Elmo.

But Piali doesn't hear him. He's stuck on his misfortune.

                    DRAGUT
            Piali. Select only soldiers who cannot swim.

Piali looks at him confused at the command.

                    DRAGUT
            Cornered rats fight desperately.

Mustapha grins in anticipation. But Piali cannot.

                    DRAGUT
            And tell all Janissaries. A reward for every
            knight's head brought to me.

                    PIALI
                (still stuck in his own thoughts)
            Portage?

EXT. JUST OUTSIDE OF TURKISH CAMP - DAY

The inland is rocky and treacherous. Garrisons of Turkish soldiers and Christian slaves carry galleys over the topography with determined fortitude. Portage. Piali watches it all.

INT. FORT BIRGU - DAY

Through his spyglass, in the tower, La Valette sees the boats crossing the terrain. He turns to Romegas.

> LA VALETTE
> Have the Maltese set up their barrier. And check
> on our floating bridge.

EXT. FORT SENGLEA SHORELINE - NIGHT

Maltese swimmers glide out just offshore of Senglea. They carry the wooden spikes carved earlier out of small tree trunks.

They plant them in the shallow, points just below the waterline. Ready to puncture anything that tries to land.

Others pound poles down and attach a chain to hold back ships from landing as well.

EXT. PENINSULA INLET BETWEEN BIRGU AND SENGLEA - NIGHT

In the inlet between the two peninsulas and their castles, a floating bridge is completed, connecting access between the two fortresses. It's made of barrels and wood.

INT. DON GARCIA'S COUNCIL ROOM - DAY

> SUPER: SICILY

Hundreds of miles away, a wearied Salvago pleads with Don Garcia and his Noblemen in their council chamber. They're noisy, arrogant bastards who won't shut up.

> DON GARCIA
> Men, I can afford to lose. Ships, I cannot.

This infuriates Salvago. But he maintains diplomacy.

> SALVAGO

Viceroy. If we tried to sail out of Malta's harbor, we would lose all our ships a hundred meters from port.

A hawk-nosed Nobleman pipes up.

> HAWK NOSE
> Why should we hazard ourselves for an Order of aristocratic knights that has blackballed our own noble sons?

The Nobles GROWL in agreement.

> SALVAGO
> (pleading)
> What about noblesse oblige?

The Nobles grumble in complaint. Don Garcia grows perturbed.

> HAWK NOSE
> The Knights of St. John are an international Order. Let others oblige.

> SALVAGO
> Viceroy. Your delay has cost us St. Elmo. It is only a matter of days before the whole of the island falls. And after it, all of Europe.

This accusation upsets Don Garcia.

> DON GARCIA
> Salvago! Dost thou bite the hand that feeds thee?

> SALVAGO
> Sir? How can we bite if we have no teeth?

Don Garcia is a torn man.

EXT. MARSA BAY SHORELINE - DAY

The portaged ships are lowered into the water by exhausted slaves. Piali tromps about irritably.

> PIALI
> Hurry, you dogs! We are losing time!

EXT. DRAGUT'S TENT - DAY

Dragut watches the galleys set into the bay through his spyglass.

Mustapha steps up.

> DRAGUT
> How do the miners advance?

> MUSTAPHA
> They will reach the walls of Birgu in several days.

Dragut looks beyond Mustapha to three mining shafts hidden behind a hill. A line of Miners carry buckets of dirt and rock out of the small openings. Their destination: Birgu.

> MUSTAPHA
> They will never suspect it with all our forces
> arrayed against Senglea.

> DRAGUT
> Soon we will smoke out this nest of vipers.

He smiles wickedly.

EXT. ST. ELMO'S FORTRESS - DAY

> SUPER: JULY 15

A huge basilisk belches a cannonball at Senglea from St. Elmo across the water. It has begun.

The walls of Senglea hold up well to the salvo.

EXT. MARSA BAY - DAY

Piali guides his ten ships of Janissaries toward Senglea.

INT. FORT BIRGU'S WALLS - DAY

Copier and his cavalry stand before La Valette. They salute.

> COPIER
> Grand Master. My men are itching for battle. Say
> the word and we will sally forth.

>   LA VALETTE
>   Your odds outside the wall are impossible. We
>   need you within.

>   COPIER
>   Forgive me, sir. But the Turks. Their base camp. It
>   is virtually unguarded.

La Valette looks at the clever Copier.

>   LA VALETTE
>   Can your horses swim?

>   COPIER
>   (smiling with pride)
>   Like otters, sir. It will be a pleasure.

>   LA VALETTE
>   Copier. War is not a pleasure.

>   COPIER
>   (sobering up)
>   Yes, sir.

La Valette pauses.

>   LA VALETTE
>   Godspeed.

Copier salutes and leaves. La Valette turns to Romegas.

>   LA VALETTE
>   Man the stations on the Fort Birgu shoreline.
>   Ready yourselves.

Before he can even finish, Romegas is gone.

EXT. FORT BIRGU - NIGHT

From a hidden position at the base of Fort Birgu, Romegas watches Copier and
his men and horses, enter the water at the castle's edge and swim for their death
mission.

EXT. FORT SENGLEA SHORELINE - DAY

On the other side of the peninsulas, Piali and his warships round the bend, Fort Senglea in view. Piali grins like a devil.

EXT. DRAGUT'S TENT - NIGHT

Dragut with spyglass sees Piali's fleet approach Fort Birgu.

EXT. FORT BIRGU - DAY

In the tower high atop Birgu, La Valette also watches with spyglass. He turns to a flagman.

> LA VALETTE
> Withdraw the men on the ravelin.

The flagman waves to the soldiers on the ravelin wall, that second castle barrier.

EXT. FORT SENGLEA RAVELIN WALL - DAY

The soldiers march back to the fort. Lift the small bridge.

EXT. FORT SENGLEA SHORELINE - DAY

Piali and his ships are almost to shore.

And then they hit the underwater spikes.

One of them pierces right into a galley, ramming it to a halt. Sailors topple. Water gushes into the hold.

Piali sees the chains and spikes just below the waterline.

Men fall into the water. One of them gets skewered on a spike. His SCREAM dies in a gurgle of water.

> PIALI
> Halt! Halt progress!

Another galley hits a chain and bounces back.

Piali turns to his captain.

> PIALI
> Get your men in the water and get rid of these
> barriers.

CAPTAIN

They cannot swim, Admiral. By your own orders.

Piali is livid with rage.

PIALI

By the beard of Mohammed! Pull aft. Circle to the
other side of Senglea!

EXT. FORT SENGLEA - DAY

The knights and soldiers wait at the castle walls. The outside ravelin barrier is
empty. The silence deafening.

And then that sound again. ULULATION of religious fanatics devoted to death.

The IAYALARS stream upon the ravelin wall. Their ladders up. They climb,
expecting resistance.

But there is none. Because there are no soldiers on the ravelin wall.

They flood the breached ravelin. Insatiable fury.

They pour down into the ditch to breach the castle wall.

Once they reach the bottom, a hundred ARQUEBUSIERS pop up from behind
castle walls and pump the wide-open Iayalars with lead from their muskets.
Sheep to slaughter. Myriads fall. The rest claw their way back up the ravelin
wall. But it's too steep.

Wildfire finishes them off, the ditch is a river of blood and burning bodies.

EXT. FORT SENGLEA - DAY

Piali's galleys turn the corner of the far side of Fort Senglea. Piali, tall and proud.

PIALI

Prepare to land!

EXT. FORT SENGLEA CASTLE BASE

Romegas, mere meters away from the landing galleys, hides beside a cannon in
the rocky lookout. He waits for the right moment.

It comes. He signals his men. Cannons roll forward.

EXT. PIALI'S SHIP

Piali sees the battery. Screams at the top of his lungs.

> PIALI
> Pull back! Pull back!

Not soon enough.

EXT. FORT SENGLEA CASTLE BASE

Romegas and his artillery are point blank. Arquebusiers fire muskets.

Cannons vomit death upon the unsuspecting seamen.

EXT. PIALI'S SHIP

Piali's ships are caught in a close range crossfire. Ships are blasted with boulders and chains hot. Masts collapse. Hulls burst. Ships sink. Men jump into the water only to drown. It's devastating.

But TWO TURKS manage to break free from the chaos. They raise their muskets and fire.

EXT. FORT SENGLEA CASTLE BASE

Romegas is hit by a double blast and thrown flat on his back. He looks down at his chest. Two large dents in his armor. The musket balls failed to penetrate.

He stands and raises his fist with gusto and glory.

> ROMEGAS
> St. Elmo's pay! St. Elmo's pay!

The others join in.

> OTHERS
> St. Elmo's pay! St. Elmo's pay!

EXT. FORT SENGLEA CASTLE BASE

The ships are sunk. Shreds of wood and debris.

Piali swims away on a piece of wood, cursing the knights and their God.

INT. BIRGU WAR COUNCIL ROOM- NIGHT

La Valette is in council with Romegas and other Bailiffs.

LA VALETTE
Retreat from the ravelin wall was a foolish tactic.

BAILIFF
We killed hundreds in the ditch.

ROMEGAS
But we lost control of the ravelin.

La Valette reflects out loud. His soul is disturbed.

LA VALETTE
We strategize with the lives of men.

Romegas watches the Grand Master closely.

LA VALETTE
Is there any intelligence on mining?

Romegas shakes his head. And then from the back of the room.

A VOICE
Grand Master!

Everyone turns. In walks Salvago, battered from his round-trip seafaring.

LA VALETTE
What news have you, Salvago?

SALVAGO
Don Garcia has promised sixteen thousand
reinforcements. -- As soon as possible.

But he is not convincing. Even to himself.

Romegas shivers.

LA VALETTE
First, Twenty-five thousand, then twenty. Now,
Sixteen.

ROMEGAS
God, stop the man before he reaches a hundred.

LA VALETTE
How soon?

Salvago shrugs in resignation.

Romegas looks uneasily at La Valette, who seems lost in his own revelation.

> LA VALETTE
> So, the time has finally arrived.

INT. FOOD PANTRY, SENGLEA - NIGHT

Starkey is exhausted. He stares at the poor around him wolfing down their rations.

He notices commotion in the streets and moves to see what it is.

Knights are marching through the streets to a gathering.

He whisks outside and gets the attention of one.

> STARKEY
> What occasion is this?

> KNIGHT
> La Valette has called a Chapter General meeting.
> The Chapel of Bones.

Darkness comes over Starkey.

INT. CHAPEL OF BONES - NIGHT

The chapel is a macabre sanctuary. Covered wall to wall with skulls and bones. Lead knights dutifully in the pews whisper amongst themselves. Romegas is there.

La Valette enters and walks up front. A hush falls over the men.

He points to the bones.

> LA VALETTE
> Behold, a cloud of witnesses. The remains of your
> brothers who fought valiantly in the past
> upholding the code of chivalry.

The knights look around. Skulls glare at them from the dead.

> LA VALETTE
> Some say it is a new world. A world of cynicism
> and despair.

And Starkey is there too, in the shadows at the back.

> LA VALETTE
> But I say dignity is alive in the hearts of those who
> believe.

The knights mutter in agreement.

> LA VALETTE
> I am proud of you. All of you.

He pauses. Difficult to go on.

> LA VALETTE
> There will be no reinforcements from Spain or
> Sicily -- or anywhere. We are entirely on our own.

A deadly hush goes over the crowd of warriors.

> LA VALETTE
> Only God can save us now.
>   (beat)
> And may God have mercy upon us.

With that, La Valette walks down the aisle and out of the Chapel.

The knights watch in silent awe.

Starkey backs away out of sight as La Valette passes.

Up front, Romegas stands.

> ROMEGAS
> Forward, soldiers! This is holy war!

The knights stand in unison and cheer.

> KNIGHTS
> Holy war! Holy war! Holy war!

EXT. CHAPEL OF BONES - NIGHT

La Valette stops outside the doors of the chapel. CHANTING in the background.
A tear runs down his proud cheek.

INT. SACRED INFIRMARY WARD - NIGHT

Selima is absorbed in the Luther pamphlet, oblivious to the GROANS of wounded around her. A shiver runs through her.

A silhouette in the doorway. It's Starkey. She hides the pamphlet.

He approaches her. A wounded soldier SCREAMS to a chaplain.

> KNIGHT
> I don't want to die! I don't want to die!

He meets her. They share a dread words cannot say.

The knight is calmed. The chaplain leaves.

They're all alone. Starkey pulls Selima out into the hall. They slide into the shadows, kiss and caress.

> SELIMA
> You have paid dearly to be with me.

With all his soul. A desperate look. A crushing embrace.

Then he pulls away. He can't look into her pleading eyes.

> STARKEY
> The fall of Senglea and Birgu is imminent.

There's nothing she can say to give him relief. She sighs.

And then, with his heart fighting him...

> STARKEY
> We two serve different gods.

She painfully hears the echo of her own words in her ears.

> STARKEY
> I thought I could live between two worlds. But
> instead, I have lost both.

Heavy-hearted, he pulls himself away.

Somehow, she knows he is trying to spare them both a far greater loss.

EXT. FORT SENGLEA RAVELIN WALLS - DAY

Dirt ramps mount the ravelin wall. Hundreds of slaves wheel cannons to the top.

But they are picked off mercilessly by rifles on Fort Senglea's wall.

INT. DRAGUT'S TENT - DAY

With the cannons of St. Elmo echoing in the background, Dragut is approached by Mustapha and a water-sogged Piali.

Dragut peers at Piali. Mustapha breaks the tension.

> MUSTAPHA
> We cannot mount the cannons on the ravelin.
> Their marksmen are slaughtering every slave we
> send in.

> DRAGUT
> Replace them with others.

> MUSTAPHA
> They are heavy losses, Dragut.

> DRAGUT
> What care I for slaves. They are Christians. Let
> them kill their own.
>   (a thought hits him)
> Engage the cannons behind lines.

> MUSTAPHA
> Pull back the slaves?

> DRAGUT
> No.

Mustapha and Piali look at each other.

> DRAGUT
> We will fill the ravelin ditch with rubble and
> bodies and use them to cross over.

EXT. TURKISH CAMP OUTSIDE FORT SENGLEA - DAY

Artillery behind Turkish lines detonate with fury.

The walls of Fort Senglea are pummeled by lead and marble.

And so are the slaves trying to place the ravelin cannons.

FAR SHOT ST. ELMO'S FORTRESS - DAY

The cannons of St. Elmo continue their volley at Fort Senglea from across the harbor. They're being pounded front and back.

INT. FORT SENGLEA - DAY

A street procession of Corpus Christi marks the holy day. Altar boys carry the host in its curtained ark, followed by church nobility and the faithful.

La Valette stubbornly leads the procession as walls all around shake from raining cannonball.

Starkey stands in the food pantry, seething at the old man's persistence.

As the procession passes, onlookers bow to the Eucharist with ritual obeisance.

Starkey stands back in the shadows, unwilling to submit.

Selima is there, seeing it all. She surprises him.

> SELIMA
> So, the Secretary is too proud for repentance.

> STARKEY
> I cannot believe in a religion of intolerance.

> SELIMA
> What is it you do believe in?

> STARKEY
> Myself. And the power of reason.

> SELIMA
> That would make you -- intolerant of religion?

Starkey moves away from her with shame.

Another explosion nearby and everyone ducks from shrapnel.

INT. MINING SHAFT SOMEWHERE UNDER BIRGU

Turkish miners dig away at the rock and dirt. Above, the MUFFLED PERCUSSIONS of battle.

EXT. FORT SENGLEA'S WALLS - DAY

Outside the walls, rubble and bodies fill the ditch.

INT. FORT SENGLEA'S WALLS - DAY

Behind the walls, knights and soldiers hide under the barrage.

But Romegas stands in the midst of the fire.

> ROMEGAS
> Damn these vile heathens! Return fire!
>
> (no response)
> I said return fire!

A Cannoneer looks confused at a fellow soldier.

> SOLDIER
> You heard what the Officer said.

ALL DOWN THE LINE

Knights brave the blasting, pack their cannons and fire away.

EXT. FORT SENGLEA'S WALLS

The knight's cannons launch their own volley onto the Turkish side.

INT. SPARSE CELL, BIRGU

Starkey flogs himself in his empty stone room. He hears the sounds of distant battle. Looks over to his sword and shield in the corner. Cannot bring himself out of despair.

He looks up to a small cross hanging on the wall. He gets up and pulls it down.

Throws his flogging stick to the floor.

EXT. TURKISH SIEGE ENCAMPMENT - DAY

Dragut is with his Turkish gunners, watching it all.

Mustapha and Piali approach him in the distance.

INT. FORT SENGLEA'S WALLS - DAY

An artillery gunner detonates his culverin cannon aimed at the Turkish lines.

P.O.V. THE FLYING CANNONBALL...

...glides through the sky overhead toward the Turkish camp.

Right toward Dragut! It hits a cannon nearby and the whole thing is blown to shreds.

Dragut is thrown by the force to the ground.

Mustapha and Piali come running.

They find Dragut, barely alive. Mustapha panics.

> MUSTAPHA
> Stop the cannons!!

Piali goes running to his commanders.

INT. FORT SENGLEA'S WALLS - DAY

Abruptly, the Turkish cannons cease fire.

Romegas stands and stares out over the wall. His men still cower behind their cannons. La Valette approaches Romegas.

> LA VALETTE
> What think you, Romegas?

> ROMEGAS
> Some kind of tragedy most likely, sir.

They continue to watch.

> LA VALETTE
> I wonder what fortune God has bestowed upon
> us.

INT. DRAGUT'S TENT - NIGHT

Dragut lies near death. A doctor tends to his head wound. An Imam MUMBLES prayer. Mustapha leans close.

> DRAGUT
> (fighting every word)
> Have - we - taken the fortress?

Mustapha looks back at Piali. He swallows.

> MUSTAPHA
> Yes. Yes, we have, sire. Slaughtered them like
> rodents.

Piali is impressed with Mustapha's guts. Dragut COUGHS.

> MUSTAPHA
> It is a matter of days, hours, and we will be done
> with these vile vermin.

> DRAGUT
> Excellent. Take Birgu -- without mercy.
>> (Mustapha grins with delight)
> Perhaps -- you will not -- foul up this siege after
> all.

Mustapha is stung by the insult. Piali, amused.

> DRAGUT
> Leave me be. All of you.

The Imam halts his CHANTING. The servants leave. Piali looks to Mustapha and they leave.

EXT. DRAGUT'S TENT - NIGHT

The two Generals exit the tent.

Two war-torn AGARS approach. With them, a soldier carrying a comrade, sick with fever.

> MUSTAPHA
> What is it, soldier?

The sick soldier spasms and falls to the ground in a seizure of grotesque contortions.

Mustapha and Piali pull back, frightened by the scene.

> AGAR
> Plague, sire. It is spreading rapidly.

> OTHER AGAR
> Our water is contaminated, Our ammunitions,
> low. It has been three months and the troops are
> demoralized by the losses.

Mustapha looks to Piali. He can only shrug in agreement.

>   AGAR
> Some fear Dragut's wound is a punishment from
> Allah.

Piali waits with interest for Mustapha's response.

>   MUSTAPHA
> Do you not submit to Allah's will, Agar? Or do
> you fight against fate itself?

The Agars are shaken. The leader gathers strength.

>   AGAR
> The Janissaries will fight no more, sire. We beg an
> audience with Dragut.

Mustapha glares at them, fuming in anger.

>   MUSTAPHA
> Dragut is dead.

Piali looks shocked at Mustapha, who seems lost in his own devious plans.

>   MUSTAPHA
> I am his successor. His dying wish was that we
> finish this battle for Dragut and Allah.

>   AGAR
> But sire...

>   MUSTAPHA
> Are you spokesmen for these Janissaries?

The Agars look at one another.

>   AGAR
> Yes, your highness.

>   MUSTAPHA
> Kneel before me.

With trepidation, they kneel. Mustapha looks to heaven.

>   MUSTAPHA
> Allah. Your warriors grow weary.

The Agars bow their heads in prayer.

> MUSTAPHA
> In place of their fearful hearts...
>
> > (silently pulls his scimitar)
> ...Please accept... their heads.

Mustapha spins in a circle. He swings wide with his blade and cuts off both their heads.

Piali is agape. The soldier stumbles back in fright.

Mustapha points at him with the authority of Allah himself.

> MUSTAPHA
> Go tell your comrades rebellion will not be
> tolerated. Dragut commanded it.

The soldier stumbles off into the night.

> PIALI
> Befitting of the mighty one, himself.
>
> > (beat)
> But Dragut's "death" may cause our soldiers to
> lose heart.

> MUSTAPHA
> Dragut's "death" will give the enemy false hope.

Mustapha stares with assurance into the night.

INT. FORT SENGLEA'S WALLS - NIGHT

TWO NIGHTWATCHMEN, stand by the walls overlooking the battlefield of Fort Senglea.

Turkish medics retract their dead. In the background, an eerie FUNERAL DIRGE permeates the Turkish camp.

One of the watchmen, turns to the other, a nervous, twitchy one named FRANCIS.

> WATCHMAN
> Didya hear? Turkish deserters told the Grand
> Master. It was that bastard Dragut. May he burn
> in hell.

FRANCIS
Turks deserting to our side?

WATCHMAN
They're barbarians, Francis. Have ya not noticed?

Francis turns white.

FRANCIS
We shall all die. Every one of us.

WATCHMAN
The Grand Master has faith in us.

FRANCIS
Easy for him to say. From the safety of a command
post.

WATCHMAN
All the same. We are noblemen.

FRANCIS
Better a live slave, than a dead aristocrat.

The Watchman turns away in denial.

WATCHMAN
I didn't hear that, Francis. I suspect you didn't say
it.

He waits for a reply. Nothing. He turns.

And Francis is gone. He's over the wall, climbing down the bricks.

WATCHMAN
Francis!

Francis turns at the bottom of the wall. Their eyes meet. No turning back. Francis sprints for the Turkish camp.

WATCHMAN
Deserter! Deserter over the walls!!

A few soldiers come running to his side to see Francis disappear into the night.

SOLDIERS
That is the twentieth one today.

INT. MUSTAPHA'S TENT - NIGHT

The traitor Francis stands before Mustapha, Piali and their Interpreter. He's winded from his escape. They inspect him curiously. Deserter -- or spy?

> FRANCIS
> They cannot hold out. The forces are amassed at
> Senglea. And Fort Birgu is almost vacant.

The Interpreter relays in Turkish. Mustapha responds.

Piali jerks a sly look at Mustapha as the Interpreter speaks to Francis.

> INTERPRETER
> Is the Sultan's harem still imprisoned in Senglea?

> FRANCIS
> Yes.

Piali enjoys watching Mustapha trying to remain stone-faced.

> PIALI
> (to Mustapha in Turkish)
> How close are the miners to Birgu?

> MUSTAPHA
> Close enough.

He barks angrily to the Interpreter, who deciphers for Francis with somewhat less ferocity.

> INTERPRETER
> The General wishes to thank you for your
> assistance.
>
> (to the guards in Turkish)
> Take him away and kill him.

Francis nods hopefully then he looks up at the Soldiers as they jerk him away to his destiny.

> MUSTAPHA
> Tomorrow, we take Birgu.

PIALI
(with subtle irony)

Such selfless devotion in protecting the Sultan's interests. I am confident Selima is only of secondary consideration.

MUSTAPHA
Your confidence will be rewarded generously,
Piali.

And Mustapha leaves irritated as Piali smiles cunningly.

INT. SACRED INFIRMARY WARD - DAY

A host of knights are gathered in the Infirmary. Around them, the injured with gunshot wounds, torn limbs and bandaged heads. All await the arrival of their leader.

In the far corner, Starkey tends to a dismembered knight in delirium. The knight looks up at him with foggy eyes.

KNIGHT
Am I in purgatory?

STARKEY
No. You are right here on earth.

The knight recognizes him through his glaze.

KNIGHT
Sir Oliver? Why are you here? The Grand Master
needs you!

STARKEY
Sssshh. You need rest.

The knight convulses. Dies.

Starkey closes his eyes in pain. He places the sheet over the dead warrior and looks out into the infirmary.

La Valette enters through the doors with Romegas. But he is not in his ornamental armor. He is outfitted as a common soldier!

The knights are aghast. He walks right into their ranks. A hush falls over the crowd.

Starkey pulls back out of sight to watch.

> LA VALETTE
>
> I want to thank you all for your dedication to this most worthy cause. The defense of Malta and the Holy Order of St. John. You have fought well. You have fought with honor. Those injured, most of all have suffered like Christ on our behalf.

Knights look at one another, tense, amid COUGHS and GROANS.

> LA VALETTE
>
> I do not suspect we will withstand a final assault. And so, I call upon all of you to remember your vows...
>
> > (he starts to choke up)
>
> And I implore both healthy and wounded, to rise up in defense of your holy faith.

Awe sweeps over the men.

> LA VALETTE
>
> I bid your courage sustain you in battle should I or any of your commanding officers be felled.

A knight steps forward.

> KNIGHT
>
> Grand Master. Why do you not wear the armor of your position?

> LA VALETTE
>
> In the end, we all stand naked before the judgement seat of God.

Over in the shadows is Starkey, soaking it all in. Moved by the speech but immobilized by his pride.

Around the corner, Selima sees Starkey. Eyes connect.

> LA VALETTE
>
> When your ammunition runs out, use sword and mace and anything you can to the last drop of

blood. And when you are dying, battered and
bloodied on the field of honor, you will remember
this day as the day you sacrificed for the right of
your countrymen in all the world to believe as
they do...

> (Starkey, ashamed in shadows)
> ...or do not. As their conscience bids them. May
> God be with us all. Let us confess our sins...

Starkey carefully watches the MURMUR of penitent knights.

INT. MINING SHAFT UNDER BIRGU -

SUPER: AUGUST 7

A TURKISH MINER holds a long string extending from the opening of the shaft
to the edge of the tunnel. Almost there. They dig furiously.

INT. BIRGU - DAY

Small gadgets lay over the ground of Birgu. They are crude seismic devices to
listen for mining. A stick with taut string and bells to sense movement
underground.

Some of them start to TINKLE.

A nearby YOUNG MALTESE BOY freezes in horror. He dashes off.

EXT. BRIDGE BETWEEN SENGLEA AND BIRGU - DAY

The boy darts across the makeshift bridge to Senglea.

INT. SENGLEA'S WALLS - DAY

La Valette stands with Romegas and his soldiers looking out on the Turkish
encampment.

Thousands are arrayed against them, ready for their blood.

Above, the sun burns hot on the barren wasteland.

Below, La Valette pulls at his armor. Sweat pours down his forehead.

Around him, the bruised and bandaged warriors from the infirmary. Some of
them can barely stand. But all of them carrying sword and shield, musket or
mace.

Paces away, The Grand Master's Guard watch him, also exhausted to the bone.

A knight pulls at his armor and mutters.

> KNIGHT
> I'm burning up in here.

> ANOTHER KNIGHT
> Cooked alive in your own personal oven.

They grumble in agreement.

> KNIGHT
> They may be barbarians, but they got one thing
> right with those silk robes of theirs.

The Maltese boy races for La Valette.

But he runs into the Grand Master's Guard, LEAD KNIGHT.

> LEAD KNIGHT
> Ho, there, boy.

> BOY
> I must speak to the Grand Master!

> LEAD KNIGHT
> Little boy! Can you not see the Grand Master is
> consulting for battle?

> BOY
> But I must speak to him! It is urgent!

> LEAD KNIGHT
> Not more urgent than the protection of your ass!

He shoves him down to the ground and the knights around him HOWL with laughter.

The boy is flustered. He sees La Valette at a distance. Too far to break for it. So, he yells.

> BOY
> Grand Master! Grand Master!

The Lead Knight picks the boy up and carries him away.

Just then, the weary knight collapses to the ground in heat exhaustion. Others bound to his side.

OVER BY LA VALETTE

La Valette hears the skirmish and looks back.

> LA VALETTE
> What goes there?

The knights frantically try to undo the fainted knight's armor.

> KNIGHT
> Heatstroke, sir!

> LA VALETTE
> Bring him to the infirmary.

> KNIGHT
> Yes, sir!

La Valette turns back to his strategy.

Out of sight of the Grand Master, the Lead Knight sets the boy down.

The angry little one watches him march away. Then a plan hits him. He scurries off.

BACK AT LA VALETTE AND HIS OBSERVATION POST

La Valette scrutinizes the tarrying pagan legions with eagle's eyes.

> LA VALETTE
> What say you, Romegas?

> ROMEGAS
> I do not figure, sir. But I fancy it is something wily.

INT. FOOD PANTRY FOR THE POOR - DAY

The boy stumbles into the food pantry, looking desperately for his one hope. No one.

He races through into the Infirmary.

INT. SACRED INFIRMARY

It's empty except for a few terminal cases. Selima tends one of them. The boy rushes in.

> **BOY**
> M'lady. Where is the Secretary?

Selima looks at him. She knows.

INT. CHAPEL OF BONES - DAY

Starkey sits in the pew at the front of the altar staring down the stone-eyed Christ on his crucifix of wood. Starkey remains at war within his soul.

The boy staggers in with Selima. She pushes him forward and stays back to observe.

> **BOY**
> Sir Oliver!

Starkey turns.

> **BOY**
> Sappers are at the walls of Birgu! They're mining!
> But no one will listen!

Starkey considers. Then spits out.

> **STARKEY**
> Prepare to meet thy maker, boy.

The boy is crestfallen.

Starkey turns away, resigned to fate.

The boy drags himself out in failure.

> **SELIMA**
> So, it is a new world. And no one can stop it.

Starkey hears the haunting voice. He spins around. She's gone.

He looks back up at the crucifix. His eyes, flooding with contempt.

And then the revelation hits him. Straight in the heart. Burns to his soul. Breaks him to his knees in sobbing and remorse.

INT. SENGLEA'S WALLS - DAY

La Valette and Romegas still watch and wait for the swarming hordes to attack.

> ROMEGAS
> They are like locusts.

La Valette looks at him in a moment of shared fear. And then from behind, GASPS from the crowd. They turn.

It's Starkey. In his full suit of armor. Repentant. Redeemed. Ready for war.

OVER IN THE CROWD OF MALTESE ONLOOKERS

Selima watches Starkey with pride and love.

EXT. TURKISH CAMP - DAY

A Messenger runs up to Mustapha overlooking the field of Janissaries hovering before Senglea. Mustapha orders Piali.

> MUSTAPHA
> Commence firing upon the bridge.

EXT. ARTILLERY ROW OF CANNONS

The Turkish gunners light their cannons and they belch fire.

EXT. BRIDGE BETWEEN SENGLEA AND BIRGU - DAY

Ball and shrapnel fall like hail on the frail bridge between the castles. Huge splashes get nearer to the floating device. A matter of minutes and it will be demolished.

INT. FORT SENGLEA'S SIDE WALLS

Everyone runs to the walls to see. Selima is among them.

INT. MINING SHAFT SOMEWHERE UNDER FORT BIRGU

The excavation tunnel is loaded to the hilt with barrels of gunpowder.

A Miner lights a long fuse and runs for his life.

EXT. FORT BIRGU WALL

Up above, the wall of Birgu stands firm. A barrier of sand and limestone.

EXT. BRIDGE BETWEEN SENGLEA AND BIRGU

La Valette, Starkey by his side, leads a regiment of men to the bridge spanning the bay.

Mortar fire all around drenches them. They race across the bridge toward Birgu.

INT. FORT SENGLEA'S SIDE WALLS

Selima watches Starkey with helpless dread. She makes a decision and pushes her way out through the crowd.

INT. FORT SENGLEA'S FRONT WALLS

Romegas stands firm at his post. Outside the walls, the Turkish multitude, restlessly await their command.

> ROMEGAS
> Ready yourselves, men!

INT. MINING SHAFT SOMEWHERE UNDER FORT BIRGU

The fuse is almost to the gunpowder.

EXT. BRIDGE BETWEEN SENGLEA AND BIRGU

La Valette and his detachment are halfway across the bridge when a cannonball hits.

The middle of the structure explodes in a fury of splinters and wash. Soldiers at the epicenter are thrown into the water.

> UNDERWATER
> The knights sink like rocks in their metal suits of
> armor.

EXT. BRIDGE BETWEEN SENGLEA AND BIRGU

The bridge is now split. A chasm divides the regiment in half. And Starkey is on the Senglea side.

He surveys the eight foot gap, bucks up and runs full tilt for the jump. He makes a flying leap and barely hits the other side.

He starts to slip into the water -- and La Valette grabs him! A shared look of gratitude and they sprint onward.

EXT. FORT SENGLEA'S SIDE WALLS

Selima arrives by the shore of the blown out bridge to see Starkey and the others hit the other side of Birgu.

She looks around and sees a small taxi boat in the lapping water.

EXT. TURKISH CAMP

Mustapha looks through his spyglass. Piali is beside him.

> MUSTAPHA
> Let us see whose God rules now.

THROUGH THE EYEPIECE

He sees the knights pile their way into the fort. His vision glides back to the blown out bridge. And then he stops.

Into view comes the very distinct form of Selima rowing a taxi boat across the waterway after the knights.

Mustapha drops his eyepiece in open-mouthed shock. His betrothed.

> MUSTAPHA
> (whispering to himself)
> Selima. No. No.

Mustapha turns to Monster, standing behind him.

> MUSTAPHA
> Retrieve my mount and follow me!

Monster jumps.

Piali looks confused at the leader who turns to him as he's leaving.

> MUSTAPHA
> Piali, finish the strategy as planned.

Piali watches Mustapha get on his horse next to Monster.

> MUSTAPHA
> I will lead the attack forces.

> PIALI
> But, Mustapha...

Mustapha is gone.

INT. MINING SHAFT SOMEWHERE UNDER FORT BIRGU

The fuse is closer. Seconds from detonation.

INT. FORT BIRGU'S WALLS

La Valette, Starkey and their men run to the aid of a unit of soldiers already in place.

They grab trumps and grenades.

INT. MINING SHAFT SOMEWHERE UNDER FORT BIRGU

The fuse hits. A thousand pounds of gunpowder FLASHES.

EXT. FORT BIRGU'S WALLS

The earth erupts in a cataclysm of destruction. The castle wall disintegrates. Crumbles like sand.

INT. FORT BIRGU'S WALLS

Inside the fort, La Valette and his soldiers are hurled to the ground by the impact.

INT. FORT BIRGU'S CITY

Selima, running through the empty streets, feels the shock wave as well.

EXT. FORT BIRGU'S WALLS

Smoke and debris cloud the air. Stone rains from heaven.

A gaping fissure in the wall presents the heart of Birgu to its invaders.

EXT. TURKISH CAMP

Mustapha, in the lead of the attack force, raises his sword in vengeance.

> MUSTAPHA
> Attack!! Warriors of Allah! Attack!!

A trumpeter blows his MIGHTY WAR HORN. A CRY OF BLOODLUST resounds through the Turkish ranks.

INT. FORT SENGLEA'S WALLS

Romegas sees the Turkish forces pour forth.

BUT NOT TO SENGLEA! They're diverting course toward the crumbled walls of Birgu!

INT. FORT BIRGU'S WALLS

La Valette's division gathers themselves into a phalanx of desperate defense.

Starkey, loyally at his Grand Master's side.

Droves of SCREAMING Turks stream down upon them in fury.

The vanguard is met by a welcoming committee. A line of musket fire, trumps, grenades. Even arrows.

Hundreds go down.

A second line of musket fire splits their ranks in confusion. La Valette is actually enjoying himself.

And then a RUMBLING by the crumbled wall. Soldiers turn.

The wall settles itself in the sinkhole. The mining shaft below caves in. A rolling wave of collapsing earth splits the battlefield in half.

Turks and knights tumble into the trench that stretches back to the Turkish camp. -- But the battle rages on.

INT. SENGLEA'S WALLS

Romegas and his division in Senglea watch in silence, powerless to help them.

He hears another HORN. Looks back out to the ridge.

A second wave of warriors appear. But this column is for Senglea. They span the distance like a pack of wild wolves.

Romegas and his men take position.

Muskets fire. Cannons bellow.

EXT. TURKISH BASE CAMP, MARSASCIROCCO HARBOR - DAY

Miles away, the long-forgotten Copier and his guerrilla forces sneak up to a hill's crest.

He looks out over the shore. Down below, the Turkish base camp rests peacefully. Copier smiles.

> COPIER
> They have been so intent upon their siege, they never considered protecting their own supplies.

INT. TURKISH BASE CAMP, MARSASCIROCCO HARBOR

A FEW GUARDS lazily keep tabs on things. On the shoreline, myriads of landing boats.

Copier and his cavalry break the crest, mad as hell, and hungry for revenge. A Turk SHRIEKS.

Copier and his squad of horsemen burst through the perimeter and spread through the camp like wildfire, muskets exploding, swords hacking. The Turks are defenseless.

Over by the shoreline, a knight prepares to torch the landing boats. Copier stops him.

> COPIER
> Soldier! We do not want them to stay.

The soldier smiles and they move on.

Outside the munitions tent, two soldiers barrel out and take a flying leap as the whole thing erupts into a fireball that rises to the heavens.

Knights give a WAR WHOOP and finish their slaughter.

EXT. TURKISH CAMP - DAY

Piali looks down upon the arena of conflict. A sound of CONCUSSION turns his head.

A mushroom cloud of black smoke ascends from the shoreline. He barks to a standing guard.

> PIALI
> Find out what that is!

The Guard salutes and runs off. Piali is filled with panic. He knows exactly what it is.

INT. FORT SENGLEA'S WALLS

Romegas and his men stave off inevitable disaster at the walls of Senglea.

The Turks have wheeled a large SIEGE ENGINE, draped with shields and sporting a makeshift draw bridge to span the ditch to the castle wall.

Projectiles ricochet off the shields. It rolls up to the ravelin wall. An invincible mobile citadel.

Romegas looks around. Sees a cannon. BARKS commands.

Knights help him wheel it to the wall.

But there is no opening for it. Just solid sandstone brick.

EXT. FORT SENGLEA'S WALLS

The Siege Engine is in place. Guns and grenades can't stop it.

The bridge starts to lower. It's bursting at the seams with frenzied bloodthirsty Turks.

INT. FORT SENGLEA'S WALLS

Romegas points the cannon directly at the castle wall itself. The knights hit the dirt.

He lights the gun. And it blows a hole right through the wall, shattering them with debris and recoil.

Romegas stumbles to his feet. Through the hole, the siege engine can now be seen.

The draw bridge hits the walls. The Turks flood in.

Romegas packs ball and powder. The skirmish pushes toward him. The cannon ignites.

KABOOM! The Siege Engine EXPLODES in a shower of Turks and shards of wood.

Without delay, Romegas runs to the wall and jumps down onto the ruins with his fellow knights.

ROMEGAS
Allah is a buggerer and a whore!

He shoots pistol, swings sword, and thrusts dagger. A one-man killing machine -
- for God Almighty.

EXT. FORT BIRGU'S WALLS

A mêlée of swords and scimitars. Starkey and La Valette, in the center of the fray,
slice away with all the strength left in them.

Starkey sees a fallen knight's sword. He grabs it and swings a twirling blade of
wrath in each hand.

A TURK sees La Valette's back and raises a pistol to take him down.

Starkey swings one of his swords and chops his hand off. The Turk screams
bloody hell. Until his head follows.

> STARKEY
> Now try to find your way to Paradise!

Out of the shadows of the surrounding walls, the frightened form of Selima watches the battle.

Starkey sees Selima. He runs over to her.

> STARKEY
> Selima! What are you doing here?!

She stands mesmerized by the mayhem. She doesn't answer him.

> STARKEY
> You must leave! Or you will die.

> SELIMA
> Perhaps that will be my redemption.

Starkey doesn't understand her.

OVER BY THE STANDARD POLE

Mustapha, Monster, and a TURKISH STANDARD BEARER push through the
castle walls.

Mustapha sees what he is looking for.

At a distance, Selima standing close with Starkey.

Absolute hatred wells up in Mustapha's eyes.

Starkey and Selima freeze when they see Mustapha.

Mustapha turns to Monster.

> MUSTAPHA
> Seize the standard.

The Standard Bearer and Monster obey.

La Valette sees them approach the flagpole that bears the flag of St. John. There's no way he's going to let them.

> LA VALETTE
> Stop those Infidels!

Several others follow La Valette, hacking and gouging their way through a gauntlet of swarming wasps.

Meanwhile, Mustapha walks determined through the fray of battle straight to his target: Starkey.

> STARKEY
> Mustapha.

Mustapha stares at him with eyes of burning contempt.

> MUSTAPHA
> (in Turkish)
> Selima. Come to my side.

She doesn't. Starkey glances at her. What will she do?

> MUSTAPHA
> (in Turkish)
> Selima!

She backs up to the corner of the wall. Mustapha looks at Starkey with revelation.

> MUSTAPHA
> (in Turkish)
> Who is this infidel swine that has corrupted you?

> STARKEY
> Sir Oliver Starkey. And I would like you to meet
> my Maker.

Starkey attacks. Swords clash.

INT. DRAGUT'S TENT

Dragut lies recovering in his sick bed. The distant sounds of war echo in his ears.

And then, his eyes pop open. He sits up, as if resurrected from the dead. He looks over and sees his battle armor beside his bed. In his eyes, a second wind of fury.

EXT. TURKISH CAMP

Through field glasses, Piali sees the Knight's flag descend.

INT. FORT BIRGU'S WALLS

The Standard Bearer pulls down the Knight's flag.

La Valette and his men greet them with furious combat.

But Monster swats knights around like they're flies.

The flag is down. The Turkish standard attached.

La Valette throws a dagger. Kills the Standard Bearer.

> LA VALETTE
>
> No quarter!

Monster turns. His sword like a windmill blade.

La Valette is fearless, God on his side.

The flag flaps halfway over the tumult. Who will triumph?

EXT. TURKISH CAMP

Piali watches the barren pole through his spyglass.

Dragut appears from behind, dressed in full battle regalia.

Piali freezes like he's seeing a ghost.

Dragut takes the glasses, looks through them. Still no standard. He throws the glasses to the ground.

Piali watches Dragut falter just a bit before grabbing his horse and leaping on his mount.

> DRAGUT
> Prepare the second wave! When the standard
> raises, attack!

> PIALI
> But Dragut!

Too late. Dragut is gone.

Piali picks up the spyglass and watches Dragut race like the wind toward Birgu's epicenter.

DRAGUT RIDING HIS HORSE

Eyes ablaze with determination. A madman on a mission. Unstoppable. Plowing through the waves of battle like a cannonball.

INT. FORT BIRGU'S WALLS

La Valette holds off Monster through sheer courageous will. But it's not enough. He'll be down in a matter of seconds.

Starkey is busy with Mustapha. He uses only one of his two blades.

Mustapha is clearly out-matched. Starkey uses both blades to whirl Mustapha's sword from his hands.

By the standard pole, a swing by Monster and La Valette is on the ground, a bleeding wounded leg. A smile on the Turk's ugly pug. Scimitar raises high. A mighty arc downward.

With a CLANG, the blade SPARKS, inches from cleaving La Valette in two. Stopped by another sword -- Starkey's!

> LA VALETTE
> God bless you, Sir Oliver.

Monster GROWLS with anger. Starkey looks up at the giant.

> STARKEY
> I will need it.

Mustapha steps forward.

> MUSTAPHA
> Kill him!

Monster starts swinging. Starkey uses both blades crossed to deflect each blow.

Mustapha, weaponless, looks over to Selima. She's gone. And he realizes he has lost her - forever. A fruitless quest.

He runs and mounts a horse and high tails it back to camp, a coward in the end.

And Starkey sees it.

La Valette gets up, limping from his wound. Turns to see...

SLOW MOTION SHOT

Dragut's warhorse breaks through the cloud of smoke and fighting. The Angel of Death.

Without slowing down, he leaps off his horse like a flying Ringwraith.

LA VALETTE
Dragut. So, you are not so dead after all.

He stands before the battered and bruised La Valette. Generals, eye to eye.

The defining moment of the entire siege. Everything has come down to this face off of two mighty warriors.

La Valette falters, his leg still bleeding.

Dragut is bleeding himself from his head wound. But he breaks the trance with a SCREAM and a rush.

They meet. Blades cross. Sparks fly.

STARKEY AND MONSTER

Back up against the wall. A whack snaps one of Starkey's swords in two.

He drops it. Dodges. Slices Monster's turban off his head. Monster SNARLS.

Starkey bolts up a wall rampart. Monster takes chase.

Starkey's armor is cumbersome. Monster catches him at the top.

Starkey barely wards off his enemy's pounding frenzy.

LA VALETTE AND DRAGUT

battle around the flagpole. With a CLANG, their blades cross against the pole and freeze, straining against each other.

DRAGUT
(in English)
Give up now and you will die mercifully.

LA VALETTE
(in Turkish)
I can only promise you justice.

In a flash, swords resume clashing.

DRAGUT
(in Turkish)
For the Sultan and Allah!

LA VALETTE
For Jehovah and his Son!

STARKEY AND MONSTER AT THE TOP OF THE WALL

Their collision of metal continues. Starkey swipes. Cuts through Monster's robe.

Starkey looks confused at his sword tip, red with blood. Monster should be dead. But he keeps coming.

Another swing breaks Starkey's last sword in half.

Starkey backs up, weaponless. Vulnerable. Monster SNARLS. Drops his scimitar. He's going to do this by hand.

He grabs Starkey and lifts him like a rag doll right over his head. 300 pounds of knight and armor, barely a problem for this monster.

He moves to the wall's edge.

Starkey sees the ground, 50 feet below. His final destiny.

STARKEY
God, forgive me.

But Monster stops. GRUNTS. Falters. Drops Starkey to the ground beside him. Staggers forward. Gropes his robe open.

Bowels bulge out of the wound Starkey had given him moments before. Monster is mortal.

He stares dumbfounded at Starkey, who watches the gargantuan topple over the edge of the wall.

He hits the bottom, 50 feet below, with a THUD. Looks up at his adversary on the wall above. He GROANS and moves, still barely alive.

Above, Starkey holds the giant scimitar.

> STARKEY
> You forgot this.

He thrusts it down, a spear splicing the air, piercing Monster right through the chest.

Monster GURGLES blood and dies.

Starkey falls to his knees, utterly exhausted.

EXT. TURKISH CAMP

Piali sees the half-raised standard pole through his spyglass. His awaited sign never comes.

Mustapha arrives and jumps off his horse and stares right into Piali's soul.

> MUSTAPHA
> Why did you not send the third wave?!

Piali is speechless. Frozen in fear.

The Guard, sent earlier, arrives, panting with exhaustion.

> GUARD
> Your highness. The smoke is from our base camp.
> Ambushed.

Mustapha is cut to the quick. He sees the distant smoke.

> GUARD
> Reports from Sciberras. Reinforcements from
> Sicily for the knights. Some say a hundred ships.
> thousands of reinforcements.

Mustapha broods in indecision.

> GUARD
> Without our supplies, we do not have a chance,
> sire.

> MUSTAPHA
>
> I know that, you fool!

Mustapha looks upon the battle. And then he makes the most difficult decision of his life. One that will forever scourge his reputation in Turkish history books.

A leader on the brink of victory, on the precipice of defeat...

> MUSTAPHA
>
> Call the trumpets. We are pulling out.

> GUARD
>
> Yes, sire!

The Guard leaves. Piali glares out at the battle.

> MUSTAPHA
>
> We will lose our heads for this.

Piali gulps in fear.

INT. FORT BIRGU'S WALLS - STANDARD POLE

La Valette and Dragut continue their foray. Blade for blade, wound for wound, they're equal.

But suddenly BELLOWING TRUMPETS startle Dragut. He looks back.

La Valette grabs his chance. Swirls his sword and Dragut's blade goes flying.

La Valette backs him up to the pole, blade to his throat. The TRUMPETS BELLOW again.

The Turks all around just stop. They just stop... Turn tails and run.

EXT. FORT BIRGU WALLS

As quickly as they invaded, they vanish. Like some huge cloud of smoke sucked back into an implosion.

The knights are left standing in the breach, swords in hand.

INT. FORT SENGLEA WALL - DAY

It's the same for Romegas and his detachment. The Turks melt away into the landscape. Romegas watches in dazed wonder.

INT. FORT BIRGU WALL

Up on the wall, Starkey sees the Turks retreat back over the hillside to their camp.

INT. FORT BIRGU WALLS - LA VALETTE AND DRAGUT

Dragut at his opponent's disposal. La Valette sees the retreat. Looks into his rival's eyes. Seventy years of priesthood and soldiering struggle for control of this warrior monk.

Finally, he steps back. Allows Dragut retreat.

La Valette turns and walks away. Sees Starkey approaching, weakly, but smiling.

Dragut bitterly reaches into his cloak and pulls out a twisted dagger. Runs for La Valette's back.

Starkey sees this and moves. He reaches down and grabs an axe from a fallen comrade's corpse.

Dragut is moments from impact with La Valette, blade poised for kill.

Starkey yells. La Valette turns.

Starkey throws the axe. It embeds into Dragut's heart. He drops to his knees before La Valette, inches from murder.

La Valette looks deep into his enemy's eyes. Two gods of war in ultimate confrontation. Only one can rule.

La Valette holds high his sword and sweeps with a mighty arc - cutting off Dragut's head. His body falls at La Valette's feet.

Starkey makes it to his Grand Master. Silence all around.

La Valette looks over the fallen. Blood mixed with sandstone. Corpses piled high.

Other knights gather around their Grand Master.

Starkey falls to his knees in prayer.

La Valette touches his shoulder with compassion. He falters from his wound. Manages to bow one knee in gratitude with Starkey.

Starkey stands. Raises his sword on high.

STARKEY
A sword for the Lord! And for La Valette!!

A bellicose CHEER erupts.

The knights hoist La Valette on their shoulders and carry their proud leader in victory.

INT. FORT SENGLEA WALL

Romegas sees the triumphant knights in Birgu. He falls to his knees thankful to God.

His men rally in praise.

EXT. MOUNTAIN RIDGE TOP

Copier and his sortie gallop to the summit of a mountaintop.

Below them, they see the swarming masses of Turks pulling out of camp and leaving.

And La Valette's triumphant procession.

And Romegas' cheering Senglea forces.

And a contented smile spreads across his face. He sallies around and they finish their ride home.

EXT. TURKISH BASE CAMP, MARSASCIROCCO HARBOR

The Turkish landing boats pull away from the decimated shoreline back to their galleys offshore.

INT. DON GARCIA'S WARSHIP GALLEY HOLD AT SEA - DAY

Don Garcia de Toledo stands proudly before a mirror in his General's uniform, strutting his splendor.

He draws a sword with vainglory. A mock battle in his little mind. The fool.

EXT. DON GARCIA'S WARSHIP - DAY

A sailor up in the mast yells down.

> SAILOR
> Ho! Malta in sight!

INT. DON GARCIA'S WARSHIP GALLEY HOLD - DAY

Don Garcia puts the sword away and stumbles up the brig.

EXT. DON GARCIA'S WARSHIP - DAY

He steps up to the bow and holds up a spyglass.

Through it, he sees the Island of Malta. And a very large force of Turkish galleys SAILING AWAY. He puts down the glass, befuddled.

INT. FORT BIRGU, MALTA - DAY

A celebration is in order. Church bells RING. Maltese fill the streets as an icon of Madonna and Child lead a procession for the Feast of Nativity.

La Valette is right there with them, smiling, receiving hugs of gratitude from the partying Maltese.

Starkey is next to him, awash with joy.

EXT. FORT SENGLEA'S WALLS - DAY

Senglea's cannons fire. But now in celebration of victory.

EXT. GRAND HARBOUR PORT, MALTA - DAY

The Great Chain is reeled back to its place. The harbor is open and free again.

EXT. VILLAGES OUTSIDE SENGLEA AND BIRGU - DAY

Villagers return to their homes, helpless buildings ravaged and plundered by battle.

INT. CASTLE DUNGEON, FORT BIRGU - DARK

Ignatius, the despicable little Inquisitor, can barely hear the noises above through his stone cell walls. He can't figure it out, so he plops back down in bitterness.

INT. SACRED INFIRMARY WARD, FORT BIRGU - DAY

Selima looks out the window and watches the festivities with a heavy heart. It's her people who lost. Her eyes fill with tears. And then she hears a familiar voice.

> STARKEY (O.S.)
> Selima.

She turns. There he is. Carrying a pile of clothes. She musters her strength. Walks to him.

Runs. They embrace in a collision of passion. A moment that touches eternity.

But something is not right. He pulls away. Hands the clothes to her.

>STARKEY
>Quickly. Put these on.

She's confused.

>STARKEY
>It is a nun's habit. You will live better in a convent
>than as a slave.

She accepts the garments. Both of them, painfully yielded to the truth. A union that could never be.

An excited crowd passes the Infirmary outside. Someone breaks inside and calls.

>MALTESE
>Everyone to chapel! La Valette's orders!

Starkey drops his head. Bound by duty. Torn by love.

>STARKEY
>I have learned much from you, Selima.

>SELIMA
>And I, you.

More YELLING outside. He looks back. Fades away.

>STARKEY
>I will never forget you.

She smiles. But her soul is ripped from her. Every bone in his body fights to stay.

But he shuts the door behind him.

Selima, solitary and forsaken, utters words unheard.

>SELIMA
>I love you, Sir Oliver Starkey.

EXT. SACRED INFIRMARY WARD, FORT BIRGU - DAY

Starkey walks away silently amidst the happy-go-lucky crowd. And then heartbreak floods over him. He BAWLS like a baby.

>STARKEY
>I love you, Selima.

He melts into the masses.

EXT. GRAND HARBOUR PORT, MALTA - DAY

Don Garcia pulls up to port in his landing boat. He glowers with pride at the welcome celebration.

But when he gets out of the boat, he looks around, searching. No one to meet him. He grabs a knight.

>   DON GARCIA
>   Knight! Where is my arrival party?

The knight looks at him dumbfounded.

>   DON GARCIA
>   I am Don Garcia, Viceroy from Sicily and Admiral
>   of King Philip's navy.

Then the knight understands.

>   KNIGHT
>   Oh. He was not expecting you, sir.

Don Garcia turns sour. The celebration rages on.

EXT. ST. CHRISTOPHER'S CHAPEL, MALTA - DAY

People stream outside, trying to catch a glimpse of their heroic deliverer.

Don Garcia approaches the mob and makes his way through the throngs of bodies.

INT. ST. CHRISTOPHER'S CHAPEL

The chapel is packed to the gills with knights who await their General.

Starkey and Copier are there, scars of battle, still fresh on their bodies.

La Valette limps in. His leg bandaged. His spirit renewed. A hush goes through the chapel.

>   LA VALETTE
>   Today, Almighty God has delivered us. Today, we
>   routed the enemy.

CHEERS and APPLAUSE. He quiets them down.

> LA VALETTE
>
> But not without the loss of far too many brethren...

OUTSIDE THE CHAPEL

Don Garcia finally makes it to the window to listen.

> LA VALETTE
>
> ...Many believed we could not survive...

Starkey is almost in tears.

> LA VALETTE
>
> ...No one came to our aid...

Don Garcia is shamed to the core.

> LA VALETTE
>
> ...It is a new world that we have saved. A world
> that no longer values the code of honor we vow. A
> world that will crown us now but will ultimately
> despise us for saving it. A new world, with a new
> god. And a new intolerance for all that went
> before it. Your names, your faces, your sacrifice
> will fade into history. But the courage you have
> shown and the dignity you have upheld can never
> be taken away.

He turns and bends his knee in pain before the large chapel crucifix.

Rapt attention in the crowd.

And then Starkey stands. He starts to sing. It's a song that will become famous throughout the Mediterranean.

> STARKEY
> (singing softly)
> Malta of gold. Malta of silver. Malta of precious
> metal. We shall never take you...

Romegas stands and joins in. Then Copier. And another knight.

One by one, until every pew and every window is filled with the sound of holy lyric.

The singing fades down and Starkey's VOICE-OVER replaces it over the visuals.

> STARKEY (V.O.)
> In the Great Siege of Malta, 250 knights of St. John
> and 8000 soldiers and Maltese lost their lives.

EXT. SULTAN'S PALACE, ISTANBUL, TURKEY - DAY

Mustapha and Piali stand in disgrace before Sultan Suleiman's throne.

Piali's wife, the Sultan's granddaughter, runs to his side. Suleiman can't decide their fate. Then, he dismisses them with a wave of disgust.

Piali stumbles down the stairs with his wife, grateful for his life. Mustapha, close behind.

> STARKEY (V.O.)
> ...The casualties of the Ottoman Empire: 30,000.
> Sultan Suleiman the Magnificent lost his rule of
> the seas, never invaded Europe and died the
> following year...

INT. KING PHILIP'S THRONE, SPAIN - DAY

La Valette kneels before pretentious King Philip of Spain. Philip presents a jewel-studded sword and dagger to the humbled Grand Master.

POPE PIUS steps forth and blesses La Valette, who bows in prayer.

> STARKEY (V.O.)
> ...We knights and Grand Master were duly
> rewarded with honors from King Philip of Spain
> and Pope Pius himself. Don Garcia faded into
> obscurity and was never heard from again...

Behind Philip's entourage, an unseen Don Garcia shies away in disgrace and dissolves into the darkness.

EXT. ROYAL COURT, ENGLAND - DAY

Proud, Protestant QUEEN ELISABETH of England smiles from her throne on high. Before her, kneels Starkey, received and absolved with heroic honors.

Behind him, the masses CHEER.

> STARKEY (V.O.)
> ...Even less-than-favorable Queen Elisabeth was
> grateful and awarded a temporary respite from
> hostilities...

INT. ST. CHRISTOPHER'S CHAPEL, MALTA - DAY

We are back to the present in the chapel as the men finish their song. La Valette is still kneeling in silent prayer.

> STARKEY (V.O.)
> ...Grand Master Jean de La Valette refortified
> Malta and died two years later -- the last, and
> greatest of knights.

La Valette raises his sword high.

In the background, the crucifix, so long defended, fades into darkness. A portent of the future.

FREEZE FRAME ON SWORD.

THE END

Deleted Scene:
Flashback to the Conquering of Rhodes

This occurs just before La Valette and Starkey meet with Dragut on Malta to determine terms of their surrender.

> LA VALETTE
> I was there in Rhodes.
>
>> (beat)
>
> A mere youth of twenty seven years.

Starkey watches his Grand Master closely. La Valette's voice-over continues over FLASHBACK VISUALS:

> LA VALETTE (V.O.)
> We were surrounded by the Sultan's forces. The
> very same Suleiman. We held the island for five
> months. But we were outnumbered ten to one...

EXT. ISLAND OF RHODES - DAY

ESTABLISHING SHOT of the island. Hillside castles surrounded by immeasurable numbers of Turks.

Galleys sporting the crimson star and crescent of Islam clog the harbor. No way out.

EXT. ISLAND CASTLE, RHODES - LATER

Smoke and the stench of death hang in the air. Hundreds of dead knights lay about. An eerie silence.

> LA VALETTE (V.O.)
> ...And when the Grand Master surrendered,
> Dragut was there. The armies of the Living God
> humiliated by devil worshippers. And in my
> heart, I knew that one day I would face him
> again...

SULTAN SULEIMAN'S TENT, RHODES - DAY

La Valette and a band of knights are under guard by Islamic soldiers. Dirty with the stain of sweat and battle. He watches with great pain the scene before him.

L'ISLE ADAM stands before a proud DRAGUT, 20s, ruthless commander of the Turkish forces.

Behind Dragut on a throne is SULTAN SULEIMAN, also 20s, young leader of the Ottoman Empire, bedecked in jewels and silk.

L'Isle Adam hands Dragut his sword and bows in surrender. He in turn, humbly presents the sword to the Sultan.

La Valette tears up in suppressed rage. How dare this pagan emperor humiliate God's own army.

> LA VALETTE (V.O.)
> ...Henceforth, I swore by the Lord Christ that if I
> became Grand Master of the Order, we would
> never surrender again. Never.

EXT. ISLAND OF RHODES HARBOR - DAY

The conquered Knights of Rhodes trudge through a gauntlet of sneering Muslim soldiers on their way to their galleys at the shoreline.

Young La Valette turns and glares up at Suleiman and Dragut standing gloriously on a hill above the departing knights.

INT. LA VALETTE'S WAR ROOM

Back to the present. La Valette's eyes are red with anger. Starkey is moved, but remains resolved.

> STARKEY
> This thirst for martyrdom. Is it courage. -- Or
> merely stubborn pride?

La Valette cannot look at him. Starkey stiffens to attention.

> STARKEY

Please accept my request for reassignment to administrative services, sir.

La Valette takes a heavy sigh.

> LA VALETTE
> I have a much better idea.

If you enjoyed reading this screenplay, check out the other scripts written by Brian Godawa available in the *Screenplays as Literature Series*:

The Last Knight:
An Historical Epic Movie Script About the Siege of Malta in 1565

Home Movies
A Family Comedy Movie Script About Time Travel and Family Dysfunction

Descent of the Gods
A Horror Movie Script About a Reality TV Show and Alien Abduction

John Brown's Body:
An Historical Epic Movie Script About the Man Who Started the Civil War

Nietzsche: A Dangerous Life:
An Historical Biography Movie Script About History's Most Infamous Atheist

Pressure Point
An Action Thriller Movie Script About Corporate Murder and Environmentalism

Double Life
A Noir Thriller Movie Script About Virtual Reality and Obsession

Noah Primeval: The Movie
An Epic Fantasy Movie Script About the Primordial World Before the Flood

AD70
An Historical Epic Movie Script About the Fall of Ancient Jerusalem

I receive commissions from links to Amazon books above.

More Books by Brian Godawa

See www.Godawa.com for more information on other books by Brian Godawa.

Chronicles of the Nephilim

Chronicles of the Nephilim is a saga that charts the rise and fall of the Nephilim giants of Genesis 6 and their place in the evil plans of the fallen angelic Sons of God called, "The Watchers." The story starts in the days of Enoch and continues on through the Bible until the arrival of the Messiah, Jesus. The prelude to Chronicles of the Apocalypse. ChroniclesOfTheNephilim.com (paid link)

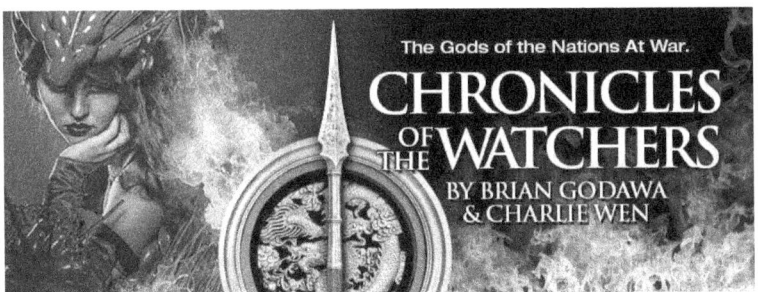

Chronicles of the Watchers

Chronicles of the Watchers is a series that charts the influence of spiritual territorial powers over the course of human history. The kingdoms of man in service to the gods of the nations at war. Based on ancient historical and mythological research. ChroniclesOfTheWatchers.com (paid link)

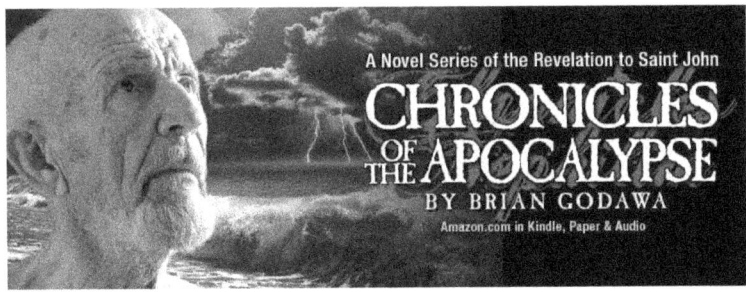

Chronicles of the Apocalypse

Chronicles of the Apocalypse is an origin story of the most controversial book of the Bible: Revelation. An historical conspiracy thriller trilogy in first century Rome set against the backdrop of explosive spiritual warfare of Satan and his demonic Watchers.
ChroniclesOfTheApocalypse.com (paid link).

About the Author

Brian James Godawa is the screenwriter for the award-winning feature film, To End All Wars, starring Kiefer Sutherland. It was awarded the Commander in Chief Medal of Service, Honor and Pride by the Veterans of Foreign Wars, won the first Heartland Film Festival by storm, and showcased the Cannes Film Festival Cinema for Peace.

He also co-wrote Alleged, starring Brian Dennehy as Clarence Darrow and Fred Thompson as William Jennings Bryan. He previously adapted to film the best-selling supernatural thriller novel The Visitation by author Frank Peretti for Ralph Winter (X-Men, Wolverine), and wrote and directed Wall of Separation, a PBS documentary, and Lines That Divide, a documentary on stem cell research.

Mr. Godawa's scripts have won multiple awards in respected screenplay competitions, and his articles on movies and philosophy have been published around the world. He has traveled around the United States teaching on movies, worldviews, and culture to colleges, churches and community groups.

His popular book, Hollywood Worldviews: Watching Films with Wisdom and Discernment (InterVarsity Press) is used as a textbook in schools around the country. His novel series, the saga Chronicles of the Nephilim is in the Top 10 of Biblical Fiction on Amazon and is an imaginative retelling of the primeval history of Genesis, the secret plan of the fallen Watchers, and the War of the Seed of the Serpent with the Seed of Eve. The sequel series, Chronicles of the Apocalypse tells the story of the Apostle John's book of Revelation, and Chronicles of the Watchers recounts true history through the Watcher paradigm.

Find out more about his other books, lecture tapes and dvds for sale at his website www.godawa.com.

BLANK PAGE

BLANK PAGE

BLANK PAGE

BLANK PAGE

BLANK PAGE

BLANK PAGE

BLANK PAGE